Out of the Shadows

Richard Johnson

All th best to the College Students

[signature]

OUT OF THE SHADOWS

GREENWATER
PUBLISHING

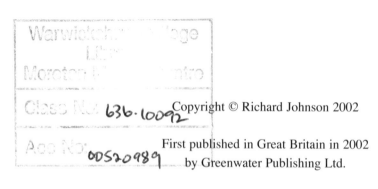
Copyright © Richard Johnson 2002

First published in Great Britain in 2002
by Greenwater Publishing Ltd.

A CIP catalogue record for this book is
available from the British Library

ISBN 1-903267-10-2

Printed and bound in Great Britain by
Biddles Limited

Greenwater Publishing Ltd.
Suite D, Pinbrook Court, Pinhoe, Exeter EX4 8JN
Telephone: 01626 852436

Photographic Acknowledgments
For permission to use copyright photographs the
author and publisher wish to thank:
The Times, Bernard Parkin, Anne Grossick, Dinah Nicholson, Mike Freeman,
David Cassap, Edward Lloyd, R.H.Wright, Les Hurley, Colin Turner
Cover: Popperfoto
Back Cover/Front Flap: Graham Flack

To my family

Contents

1.

Introduction
Deja Vu in Devon

Jump jockeys, they say, must be prepared for anything. In a precarious profession, this is a good maxim to work by. Even in my most pessimistic moments, though, I could not have anticipated the tricks fate had in store for me recently. Work on this book began while I was recovering from one broken leg and ended just after I had suffered another. To have the impetus and ambitions of one season undermined by injury was a hazard of the territory but for it to happen again in the very next season seemed harsh even by the standards of this unforgiving job. A second period of three months inactivity, with all the boredom and frustration that goes with it, was not a happy prospect.

At times such as this, the sessions of self-analysis, the endless what-ifs, are usually counterproductive but that does not mean they are easily avoided. In the hours and days following this second setback, I not only reviewed the incident countless times, fretting that I might have done something differently, I also allowed my mind to linger over how things might have turned out if this had not happened. Would I have ridden 200 winners in a season for the first time? Would I have given A.P.McCoy a real run for the championship? Sadly, these have to be filed under things we shall never know.

I was entitled to be full of hope. It was late October 2001 when I broke my leg for the first time and I had ridden 81 winners that season. Second time around, it was late August 2002 and I was already on 73 - admittedly, more than 20 behind the champion but still comfortably ahead of my previous best. My 73rd winner had been secured that very afternoon and I had been confident of adding to it in the race that brought my downfall.

It was Bank Holiday Monday in south Devon. Newton Abbot, close enough to the beach resorts of Torbay to attract a tourist crowd, had its attendance boosted further by the possibility that A.P. would ride the four winners he needed to overtake Richard Dunwoody and become the most prolific winner in National Hunt history. Sadly, I gave everyone something quite different to talk about on the way home.

I had gone there with a decent book of rides. I won the claiming hurdle, which was a bit of a surprise. I thought I might win both the chases on the card but I won neither. In the first of them, my mount pitched on landing at the second last and it was all I could do to stay in the saddle. In the second, I was three lengths clear going to the last, and got no further.

Lincoln Place was the name of the horse. Like Ilico, my ill-fated partner the first time I broke my leg, he had plenty of ability and I had no concerns about his jumping. He had won his two previous chases, he was a worthy favourite and he had done everything I asked of him in this race, stalking the leader and taking it up on the final turn. I did not look over my shoulder but I sensed my only real pursuer, a horse called Ricko ridden by my pal 'Chocolate'

Thornton, was still close enough to pose a threat. For that reason, I made no attempt to fiddle the final fence. It is not in my nature to be cautious when there is a race to be won. Given the same circumstances again, I would do nothing different. I did what comes naturally, seeing a decent stride and squeezing Lincoln Place into one last jump.

There are times, as a jockey, when you fear the worst - maybe you are on a bad stride, or simply on a dodgy horse. It wasn't like that here. The stride was good, the momentum positive but suddenly it was all going wrong and the horse had not taken off and then I remember very little else.

I don't remember hitting the ground. I have no recall of the horse rolling on me. I'm told I lay there for 15 minutes, being treated, but almost all of that has been blanked from my mind, like drawing a net curtain over the incident. Probably, I had hit my head in the fall and was slightly concussed. Possibly, that was even a good thing. All I remember clearly is the pain, much worse and more intense than the first time. This was instant, searing pain, high up in the same right leg and so bad that I think I knew immediately it was broken. I am aware, even now, of what my own thoughts were, and they were grim thoughts, but I am aware of little else except the moment when the doctor and ambulance staff tried to straighten the leg - as I know they had to do - and I screamed.

I am told that a crowd of onlookers stood on the rails, silently observing this ghastly scene, and that they applauded as I was finally lifted into the ambulance. It was lost on me, not least because I had been pumped full of sedatives and painkillers. The journey from the course to the hospital barely registered, bar a fleeting memory that the driver seemed in a tearing hurry, and although there were fully five hours between the fall and being wheeled into the operating theatre, in my mind it might as well have been five minutes.

I woke at two in the morning and suffered a moment of blind panic. I could not feel my leg, could not feel either leg. What had they done to me? Slowly, reality dawned, along with a faint memory of being told that they would double the anaesthetic below waist level. Though my top half had woken up, the bottom half was still completely numb. I breathed again. Then I started counting the days until I could ride again.

To many, this will seem strange. After all, I was fairly beaten up, sore about the shoulders and the ribs and the head quite apart from that confounded right leg. But riding over obstacles is what I do, not just for a living but for a life. It is what gets me up in the morning, what gives me the full range of human emotions. I hardly dare think what I would do without it and I have no intention of trying. Just get me back in the saddle, the quicker the better.

I was out of hospital in two days, walking on crutches and without even a plaster on the fracture. One thing in my favour was that I knew the ropes, knew what to expect from the recovery schedule, how fast I could push things in the gym and the swimming pool, how soon I could realistically set a date for my first ride back. It was a consolation of sorts, as was the knowledge that I ride for good people, trainers who will not whip round and run in the other direction when something like this happens. They tell me the horses will be there for me when I am fit again, and I believe them. In return, I can only assure them, and everyone else, that none of this will deter me. The dreams are all still there, despite the nightmares of late, and I will be back to chase them as soon as human recovery permits. It's what I do. It's what I love.

2.
Herefordshire Heritage

The lifestyle of the modern jockey is hectic, demanding and constantly in the public eye. There are not many chances to step off the merry-go-round and change the pace, but whenever I get one I know exactly where I want to go. Home is in Herefordshire, the far side of the county town, heading for the welsh borders, and life is lived a little more slowly there. This is farming country and farmers work long hours themselves but the environment is somehow more relaxing, good for the soul. When I am finished with this crazy, volatile but endlessly exciting racing game, I will go back to Herefordshire and enjoy the atmosphere at closer hand, hopefully with some mares and foals around me for company. For now, it is a bolthole, full of happy times and fond memories.

My parents, Keith and Sue, farm on either side of a narrow lane between Bridge Sollers and Madley. Except when tractors and farm vehicles are chugging down the lane (the bridge at the end is the only Wye river crossing between Hereford and Hay) it is so quiet that nothing disturbs the birdsong. These days, Mum concentrates much of her time on training eight or ten racehorses and has recently converted an old cowshed to make additional boxes. Dad runs the farming side, though I reckon many afternoons are spent in front of the racing on television. I may have made my name in the sport but it is a passion to most of the family. My other grandfather, on Mum's side, also had a permit to train, quite apart from being a joint master of foxhounds, near Leominster. He too, was an inspiration to me. The first racehorse I sat on belonged to him and he was always so supportive of my dreams. Sadly, he died when I was only ten. Only my brother, Nick, showed no interest in horses. Farming has always been his thing, though he does enjoy a social day out at the races.

Many people may look back on their childhood through rose-tinted spectacles but I'm still young enough to recall mine pretty accurately and I could not have asked for anything happier. Rural Herefordshire is an idyllic spot for kids to grow up in, especially if they have an interest in horses - and mine developed at an early age. Although Dad was race-riding as an amateur at the time, the first and biggest influence I had was his father - my grandad, Ivor Johnson. He didn't try to teach me about riding, much less about racing, but simply through watching and following him, as I did through a number of years, he transmitted the sheer enjoyment that horses can offer. And that was quite a start in life.

The great thing about grandad was that he always seemed happy. His wife, my gran, did everything for him around the home - they were as old-fashioned in this respect as in every other - and, from a grandson's perspective, he just never seemed to have a bad day. One of the worst days of my life was the day he died, the afternoon after my 21st birthday party in July of 1998. I'd had the party at home, on the farm. It was a wonderful occasion and grandad had been in great form. He was 72 years old but you would not have known it. I have pictures of him that evening, the life and soul of the gathering, and he was the most reluctant of all to bring the night to an end. It was 3am when he left to go back down the lane to his own farm in Bridge Sollers, and I never saw him again. The following day, he took gran and her sister out for Sunday lunch. On the way back they were in involved in an accident and grandad was killed. Gran (Mary Johnson) lives alone in a house at the end of our drive now, and her home is full of pictures of grandad and the horses he trained.

It is a great regret of mine that he didn't live to see my first Cheltenham festival winner on Anzum, eight months later, but whether he knew it or not he had helped me to attain that goal as much as anyone. He trained my first winner, of course, in the family pet Rusty Bridge, and put me on a few more besides, but it was his gentle manner with people and horses that made the biggest impression on me.

Grandad was a farmer through and through. Each summer, he would drive one combine harvester and Dad would drive the other - that's how they were until he died. He never thought of retiring. He was not a man who could just sit back and watch other people do the work, he had to be active. That included riding out every day, on everything from flighty three-year-old fillies only recently broken in to hoary old steeplechasers who had been around before I was born. He trained under permit himself until handing the licence on to Mum and his biggest winner as a trainer was also Dad's biggest as a jockey, when Bridge Ash won the Midland Grand National in 1982. Bridge Ash was a home-bred mare and, like the dynasty she was to throw, she needed extreme distances to be seen at her best - four miles round Uttoxeter was right up her street and I can picture Dad pushing away on her, just as I was to do many times in later years on her first foal, Rusty Bridge.

I can picture grandad now in various situations but, in my mind, he always looks the same. He was the epitome of a Herefordshire farmer, with rosy cheeks and a slightly rotund shape, yet I've seen pictures of him in his mid-thirties and he was almost painfully skinny, probably weighing about eight stone.

The artist's impression I have of him on my lounge wall at home, wearing a shirt and tie under a battered old tweed jacket, is exactly as my mental picture dictates he always looked and dressed. His smartness was a good influence on me but, in truth, those jackets had taken such a hammering over the years that they must have been in a dreadful condition. The tie, though, was always neatly knotted, no matter the circumstances - I can't even remember him riding out without one. My picture of him on horseback recalls how long he rode, his feet right down through the irons, clad either in wellingtons or his old market boots. His old hunting saddle was like a lump of lead and he would go on using it until it fell apart, then go to a farm dispersal sale and find another ancient one that would see him through two or three years. He was never one to waste money, one more thing that rubbed off on me.

I remember vividly how relaxed he always was on a horse. He only ever seemed to have one hand on the reins and the other would be swinging casually by his side. He never carried a proper stick but, as he was walking his horse down the drive, he would reach up and pull a small branch off a tree. He'd never hit his horses, just flick at them to keep their attention focused, and to me they seemed to respond to his every move. Grandad never did ride under rules but, at the age of 40, he decided to take up riding in point-to-points. I think he only did it for fun and recreation, rather than through any sudden unfulfilled ambition, but I'm told he kept at it for a number of years and thoroughly enjoyed it.

In the locality, grandad was very well-known and immensely liked - to my, admittedly biased eyes, it is hard to think of a single reason why anyone would not like him. Everything he stood for was traditional and old-fashioned and doubtless he was very set in his ways, but I never saw him try and push his views on other people.

He only ever had one or two racehorses at a time and he trained them in the most laid-back way imaginable. Next to his old farmhouse, a typically mellow Herefordshire building, was an old stone yard with two stables. Most of the time, the horse, or horses, would be free to wander around this yard as they pleased - and, because of it, they seemed as happy and relaxed as their trainer. Nobody could change grandad's training methods, which were as homespun as you could imagine. He used to take his horses out twice a day and there was no question of giving them a five-furlong canter and then putting them back in their boxes. He would ride out in the morning and go around all the sheep, so the horses might actually be out for three hours. Then, in the evening, he would tack them up and go out again. Not exactly similar to the methods of Martin Pipe but it suited grandad and seemed to suit the horses - considering their modest pedigrees, they won their share of races.

I had a pony from the age of about six (he's still around now, giving faithful service to one of the neighbours) and, every weekend, I would ride him from our farm up to grandad's house. I got into the habit of riding right up to the porch, reaching forward and rapping on the door with my stick. Gran would come out for a chat about this and that, while Grandad, if I'd timed it right, would tack up a horse and ride back with me. On Sundays, I would ride up there for lunch, which Gran loved to cook for us boys, and if Mum and Dad were busy, or away for the afternoon, I would enjoy spending the whole day up at Bridge Sollers. It was a gentle, undemanding and utterly happy way to spend a childhood day and, at the time, I thought such days would never end. Once I was old enough, grandad took me hunting. He'd load two horses - including my pony - into an old box and we would just set off for the day. It was a great adventure for me but the riding, and jumping, was no doubt educational, too.

Although I was aware of Dad going off to ride in races (and occasionally of going with him), to my infant eyes he was the busy farmer and grandad the one who spent his time with horses. When I was eight, Dad had begun to talk of giving up race-riding, not least because he was finding it increasingly hard to find the time and make the weights. But then something happened that made that decision for him, and threatened to change all our lives forever.

The day it happened, I have a clear memory of sitting in my classroom at the Cathedral Prep School in Hereford, doubtless wishing myself out in the fields with my pony. The school's secretary burst in unannounced, which plainly meant there was a drama, and after a hurried conversation between her and my teacher, I was asked to accompany them outside, where a car was waiting with Mum and an aunt sitting inside. Briefly, Mum explained that there had been an accident on the farm and that Dad was in hospital. I don't remember feeling any great sense of shock, nor of being very inquisitive to find out the details. Possibly, I was just pleased to be missing school but, on the whole, I am glad I have no better recall of what was happening. Piecing it all together later, it was a gruesome experience for Dad, and inevitable stressful for Mum, too.

The accident was the sort of freak happening that can occur around a farmyard. Basically, Dad was squashed by a pallet of fertiliser and it left him with serious injuries to his back, pelvis and legs. But he was lucky, in the sense that it might have been very much worse. For a week after it happened, the hospital feared he would not survive. Mum spent most of her time there but we boys were not allowed to see him. Finally, as he came off the critical list, the doctors warned that he would probably never walk again. With all these dire bulletins emerging from the ward, I can hardly imagine what Mum was going through but the worst of it was kept from Nick and me and I don't think we fully understood what was going on. It was only in later years that I learned there had also been great concern about his mental condition. He had been talking in his sleep, telling the dog to round up the sheep. It worried the nurses and led them to believe he might have sustained some form of brain damage but, on reflection, it was probably just Dad's way of worrying out loud about what was happening back at the farm.

It was three months before he came home, and then it was just for a few days over Christmas. He was allowed out in a wheelchair and I remember Nick and I mucking about in that chair, quite carefree, because we had that childlike faith that our Dad was indestructible and everything would be okay. Looking back, I'm sorry for Mum and what she had to go through, though knowing the neighbourhood I'm sure there were any number of volunteers to help out in the emergency. Grandad, I feel certain, took full control of the farm work in that calm and unhurried way of his.

Dad still has very little feeling in one of his feet, and the hobble is still evident, but given the circumstances and the concerns that ensued, he is a fortunate man. Amazingly, he even went back to race-riding some years afterwards, though only on a few horses and largely, I would guess, to satisfy himself that he could still do it. By then, anyway, there was a younger Johnson straining at the leash, eager to be set loose on the racing game.

Early in my teens, my heart already set on being a jockey, I would get up early every day in order to ride out for Mum. It was no hardship to me; when there was a horse to be ridden the problem for my parents was keeping me in bed long enough to get a reasonable sleep. Mum had a horse called Spend Easy, who ran in point-to-points and occasionally in hurdle races, and I was allowed to take him out at 7am and meet grandad, who would be on board Rusty Bridge. We'd do a canter up on the hill, then I would take the horse back to our farm and Mum would drive me in to school in Hereford - sometimes no more than five minutes late. My timekeeping caused a few problems with the teachers at first, as tends to happen in well-run academic establishments, but I think they soon realised they were fighting a losing battle. They stopped having a go at me, realising I was never going to change and that my teenage priorities were different from those of many other kids. I was active enough in other areas - I played rugby and cricket at school and if I set my mind to it I was not the worst student in the world - but horses, and the distant prospect of race-riding, eclipsed all else in my mind. I hope, if they have followed my career to date, the people who taught me and put up with my regular lateness feel in some way vindicated for their tolerance.

Grandad was well into his sixties by then but there was never any question of him thinking the time might have come to stop riding. He was one of those men who would have withered away if he'd given up on his lifelong routine and I suppose the one blessing of his wretchedly premature death was that he never suffered the misery of feeling old and helpless. Far from it, in fact. As soon as I was able, I was badgering him to let me ride Rusty Bridge in races and I think this new family challenge gave him a fresh lease of life.

The saga of Rusty Bridge is told elsewhere but one race he ran is relevant to this section, because it brought the only outburst of temper I ever saw in Grandad. He was such a mild-mannered man that I remember it coming as a huge shock to me, so much so that I was reduced to complete silence. It happened at Stratford, in the Horse and Hound Cup, and I think the reason was that it was a race he so badly wanted to win but had always eluded him. The fact was that it just wasn't the right track for Rusty, who needed long straights and stiff finishes to be seen at his best, and after two-and-a-half miles I was tailed-off last. I pretty much gave up on him after that, knowing we couldn't possibly be placed, and Grandad did not take kindly to this. He loved his horses to compete, to be ridden out to the line, and he told me with a fierce look and a few choice words that I had let him down. There were family ructions for half-an-hour or so, before peace was restored and the episode put behind us, but it was such an unexpected event that I have always remembered it.

I think he was approaching 70 when he had a three-year-old filly at home, a real horror to ride and almost completely devoid of ability. I rode her once in a race, a six-runner novice hurdle at Hereford, where two pulled-up and I still only finished fourth. That's as good as she was and I saw very little prospect of her improving but grandad was not a man to give up easily. One morning, as he was riding her out of the farm, she reared up, unseating him, then fell on top of him. Grandad was not wearing a riding hat and this was no careless omission. To the best of my knowledge, he had never worn one in his life and no matter how many people offered to buy him one, or how much we pleaded with him, he just would not do it. Old habits died very hard with grandad. Somehow, his head escaped intact from this tumble with the filly but he broke four ribs and was in hospital for a week. Typically, no sooner was he back out than he started riding the same filly out again, determined to prove who was boss. He never did win a race with her but he did calm her down, a triumph in itself. Grandad was that sort of man, a good influence on all around him, and I miss him still.

David Nicholson

3.
The Duke

David Nicholson

My first impressions of David Nicholson were probably no different to those of every other teenager who ever turned up at his yard looking for a job. I was scared. He was a big man in every sense - big in racing, big in stature - and his personality seemed to bulge out of his clothes. There was also the worrying fact of his reputation for having a short fuse and being generally difficult to get along with. There were those in racing, I knew, who couldn't stand him, whether through jealousy, bad experience or simply on rumour, but my upbringing had impressed two old-fashioned principles upon me - speak when you are spoken to and judge as you find. Both were to come in handy. It has not been a totally serene relationship - with 'The Duke', I'm not sure that's possible - but I can't remember a single bad day in the years I worked for him and I am genuinely glad to still have him as a friend and mentor in what is laughably called his retirement - he actually manages to make himself as busy and audible as ever.

He taught me a great deal about how to get on in racing and a whole lot more about the traditional methods of training. By this, I don't just mean the routines of the horses but of the entire yard. David had learned from his legendary father, 'Frenchie', and according to those who should know he implemented his methods pretty faithfully, placing great emphasis on discipline, organisation and generally high standards all round. It might sound a bit po-faced but, in fact, it was anything but, because the man had a sense of humour. Life at Jackdaws Castle was not a picnic, but it was good fun.

He imposed his sense of standards on all the lads in the yard. When riding for him, he insisted we wore a shirt and tie, but he did not stop there. Even if you were simply leading up a horse at the races you were expected to dress smartly and look tidy. He wouldn't have any of his lads wearing an earring and stubble was another pet hate. Hair was supposed to be respectably short and Robert Thornton's blond locks sent him into a regular moan. Just to irritate 'The Duke', 'Chocolate' once ignored his warnings for four weeks, but when the boss threatened to take him into his office and cut it himself, he gave in meekly.

I've only once seen the 'Duke' at the races without a tie and that was on such a boiling hot day that he would probably have exploded with one on. It's easy to mock, to think such codes are old-fashioned, but I have come to believe the example is a good one. I look around now at others in racing who look pretty untidy and wonder what impression they are giving to people who are, after all, potential employers. It doesn't take a lot of effort to look smart and feel better about yourself. So that's one good habit Mr Nicholson got me into.

Fundamentally, I think he always enjoyed having young people around. Perhaps it was his own advancing age and the fact that we kept him feeling younger but I think he got a lot of pleasure out of the involvement in everything we did. He didn't approve of The Plough, or indeed any of the other local pubs we frequented, so our Saturday nights out turned into an elaborate pretence. After racing, a group of us - usually including messrs Thornton, Massie, Aizpuru and Johnson - would ritually sneak out of the yard in one of our cars. The problem was that the Duke's house had to be passed on the drive out and, if he saw us, he would always wave us down and demand to know where we were going. Usually, the rehearsed answer would be that we were going to the late-night shop in Stow to stock up on some provisions. I don't think for a moment he ever believed us, especially as our 'shopping' trips took about three hours and we would return in conspicuously high spirits.

As I got to know him better, he would regale me with stories from his own days as a jockey - the overnight stops in London with such cavalier characters as Terry Biddlecombe and Josh Gifford for company. They would drink champagne, eat seafood and spend a decadent night in the Turkish baths in Mayfair, then get on the train north to ride at Doncaster. Of course, they were different times, there was less racing and the whole atmosphere around the game was more relaxed, but I think the 'Duke' loved the lifestyle so much that he wanted us to get plenty of enjoyment out of our riding days, too, and was just intent on looking out for us to make sure we didn't go off the rails.

It would be wrong to paint too soft a picture of him. Of course, he would issue plenty of bollockings - that was part of the ritual - but so long as he could see you were trying to do as he asked, he would do anything for you. For example, I got in trouble for my whip use on a few occasions early in my riding career. I think the 'Duke' probably agreed with most of the bans, when they were handed out, but that did not stop him taking it up with someone at the Jockey

Club and telling them in his usual, hectoring way that they should be doing far more to help me. Sometimes, I got to wishing he would stop going to such lengths to support me - I felt slightly embarrassed and began to wonder if I might lose rides through it - but it was still great to know the boss was fully behind me.

One area in which he was not very supportive was my driving. I think he probably believes to this day that I tried to kill him one day. We were heading for the races with the Duke and Alan King as my passengers and I overtook something with, perhaps, a shade too little room for comfort. The Duke was apoplectic and I'm slightly surprised he ever let me drive him again. His opinion of my skills at the wheel had doubtless been coloured by the fact that I had two accidents in my early years with him. The first time, I left the car in a field after snapping a telegraph pole. On the other occasion, I landed in a ditch behind a stone wall, having gone off the road in thick fog. I was late for first lot at Jackdaws and, unharmed by the prang, I rang 'Choc' to come and pick me up. He was probably looking for a written-off car and couldn't see it because it was behind the wall - anyway, he drove straight past me in the fog and we were seriously behind schedule by the time we finally linked up and got back to the yard, just in time for an already simmering trainer to take a call from the local police, asking if Mr Johnson knew that his car was upside-down in a ditch. The Duke pretended to be angry with me but I couldn't take him seriously - I genuinely think he was just relieved I was OK.

While the boss would not think twice about bellowing at any of us in the yard, or up on the schooling grounds, he was far more sensitive when it came to criticising our race-riding. His reputation for boiling over was such that I did not know quite what to expect when I started riding for him. I worried about it for a while.

Inevitably, I was going to mess up sometimes - would he shout at me in front of the owners? Well, he never did that once in all the races I rode for him, and it certainly wasn't because I managed to avoid making mistakes. If I'd been tactically naive or technically clumsy, he would smooth things over at the races, deal with the owners himself, then tell me the error of my ways, either in the car or back at the yard in his office. He'd be firm, leaving me in no doubt what I had done wrong, but he'd never tear me to shreds, let alone humiliate me in public. For all that people say about his bombastic ways, he does have a genuinely caring nature.

I understand the late 'Frenchie' Nicholson's yard in Cheltenham became known as something of a jockeys' academy - Pat Eddery was probably its most famous graduate - and the 'Duke' continued in the same style, educating and improving several generations of jump jockeys, including such champions as Peter Scudamore and Richard Dunwoody.

I've no idea what he thought of the 15-year-old Johnson when he turned up on his doorstep for the first time but I do know I was quivering with nerves. David was still training at his old yard in the cotswold village of Condicote at the time and had agreed to Dad's request to give me two weeks' work in the school holidays. I'd seen him before, of course, but generally on television, when he looked a giant to me in his familiar sheepskin coat. In the flesh, he was not as big as I'd expected but his character came across as very much larger than life. I buttoned my lip and settled down to two weeks of subservience - though it was anything but an ordeal. I don't think I ever did have any reservations about wanting to be a jockey but, after that fortnight, I could think of little else.

I was taken on as soon as I left my Hereford school in 1993. 'The Duke' had moved into Jackdaws Castle now, near the village of

Temple Guiting, and these were exciting, ambitious times for everyone connected with the yard. I spent the first three years living in the lads' hostel and, inevitably, going through the processes of initiation. One tradition was that the young lads were to be stripped and coated in clay on their birthday. There was no keeping the date to yourself, it simply didn't work, and when my 17th came around I stupidly decided to try and outrun my would-be captors. It was a hopeless cause, of course. They had planned the 'present' for straight after evening feed time and my idea of making a rapid escape back to the hostel was stymied - they had locked the door and hidden the key. As I sprinted away in search of alternative cover I ran straight into Mark White, who has since moved on to be head lad for Kim Bailey. Now, Mark was never going to make a jockey - at six feet two inches tall and with shoulders to match he was much more the rugby type. Certainly, there was no escaping his clutches and he simply picked me up and hauled me back to face the music. At least I escaped the embarrassment that had confronted two of the other lads a fortnight earlier. 'Chocolate' Thornton and Richard Burton had just suffered the coating treatment when the boss marched into the yard. He was not seeing this for the first time, I'm sure, but neither was he inclined to let it pass without comment. Loudly mocking them for a couple of fools, he instructed them to go and wash themselves down - not in the hostel, because it would make a mess, but with the hosepipe in the corner of the yard. Quite apart from doubling the public humiliation, the hosepipe also spurted out freezing water and, even in midsummer, it had an embarrassing effect on the teenage torsos.

Both Mark and Gordon Clarkson, who is now assistant trainer to Richard Phillips, have shown the enduring benefits of learning under such a good tutor as The Duke. I have seen Gordon instilling some Nicholson-type values at the Phillips yard, while 'Chocolate' tells me that Kim Bailey's operation in Northamptonshire is all the better for the set routines being introduced by Mark. I'm sure there are some assistants and head lads who just share the impatience of the average lad and get the jobs done as quickly as possible but every successful yard works on the abiding principle that the horses come first. That was the message drummed into us every day at Jackdaws and I feel privileged to have worked in such an environment, though I certainly didn't appreciate at the time how right the boss was about so many things.

The Duke had a great way of schooling horses. Loose schooling was not widely fashionable at the time and he certainly never indulged in it. Instead, he would work slowly and methodically, schooling every horse over the smallest obstacles until he was satisfied of their confidence, then moving them up to mini-hurdles and so on. Progress was steady, calculated and never rushed. I see a lot of yards cutting corners these days, much of it through staff shortages and the need to maximise available hands, but the Duke would never be hurried. He was always absolutely adamant that everything must be done as he prescribed and, looking back, I think it was demonstrably the right way for the horses, even if it might now be considered economically unsound. At the time, it seemed there was nothing very scientific about it at all but I see so many other yards now that seem unable to do the basic things so well.

Not that Jackdaws always operated with military precision. There was one infamous morning, indeed, when everything that could go wrong duly did. Nothing infuriated the Duke more than loose horses on the gallops - it used to drive him wild and he would roar at everyone in sight. Just occasionally, though, accidents will happen in the best-regulated team. We had a horse in the yard called

Silver Wedge and he was wild, to put it kindly. A two-year-old on the flat, he had jumped the running rail at Sandown, which takes a bit of doing. He came to us as a juvenile hurdler and was still headstrong, so always had a lead in his work. On the day in question, though, the head lad had a mental block and directed one of the girls to lead a group of horses on Silver Wedge. It was an invitation to equine anarchy. Halfway up the gallop, he had had enough of subordination and whipped round, depositing his rider on the deck, before setting off back towards the stables, scattering the rest of the string as he did so. Those of us bringing up the rear took shelter and watched, trying not to laugh too obviously as horse after horse was spooked. At least six riders were unseated and there were loose horses everywhere. It was carnage. Alongside me, 'Shav' Aizpuru was laughing so much his horse reacted to the din by whipping round and so he, too, was on the floor. At this point, the cavalry arrived in the shape of the Duke's Land Rover, slewing to a halt and releasing a trainer almost incoherent with rage. He bellowed at no-one in particular with the unfortunate result that those horses so far undisturbed were scared witless and two more riders hit the deck.

It was now like a spoof cowboy film and it took some while for horses and riders to be reunited and for the Duke to regain his composure. Eventually, we all made it to the top of the gallop, where Gerry Hogan's horse spooked once more and he was off again. Deleting the expletive, the Duke yelled: "I might have known that one more idiot would come off and it had to be you, Hogan." There was a bit of history here, you see. Gerry was not a bad jockey and rode his share of winners for the yard but for some reason he always bore the brunt of the Duke's temper. We all loved schooling mornings, because we knew that if bollockings were being handed out, it would be Gerry who got them - it just became a routine. We were all gutted when he left.

Fred Hutsby was another to get more than his share of earache from the guv'nor. I spent a year sharing a room with Fred and would not have swapped it for the world. He was terrific company, if a little exhausting, because when the rest of us were flaking out after a hard day in the yard, Fred was flexing his muscles and dashing off for some exercise. He was the most hyper-active lad I've ever come across and played every sport going, some of them very proficiently. What he was never going to be, though, was a top jockey. On the gallops, he would regularly cause chaos by bombing to the front of the string on a horse he was supposed to be working in behind. "Mind out, I'm coming through," he would shout, though only half as loud as the trainer then shouted at him. Fred would unwittingly come out with such funny remarks and you would never find anyone to say a bad word about him. The Duke exploded at him many times but it just passed over his head.

Fred's father had put a horse called Mighty Moss in the yard, specifically for Fred to ride in races. We didn't know if the horse was any good but the whole yard knew that Fred was not God's gift to race-riding, so when the Duke entered two for a 'bumper' at Huntingdon there was never any question of thinking that Mighty Moss would finish in the same county as the well-regarded Potter's Gale. Bob Massie was down to ride that one and the two jockeys travelled to Huntingdon together, driven by the then assistant trainer, Alan King. I suspect Alan had backed Potter's Gale - certainly, many of the lads had done - and he apparently kept stressing in the car: "Fred, you can do what you like on your horse, just keep out of the way of Potter's Gale." Well, he followed those instructions alright and Bob never saw his stablemate until he came flashing past on the run-in. The Nicholson yard had first and second, though not in the order anticipated.

Mighty Moss, of course, turned out to be a very decent sort and Fred had the distinction of riding the family horse at three successive Cheltenham Festivals - no-one can take that away from him. Mind you, he would insist on having his say. Fred's idea of race tactics was to jump off and go as fast he could for as long as his horse could gallop. Occasionally, with a horse as good as Mighty Moss, the simple ploy worked, but when it came to contesting the Sun Alliance Hurdle against an Irish hotpot called Istabraq, the Duke ordered him to show a little more restraint. Mighty Moss ran the race of his life to finish second, beaten a bare length, and in the winners' enclosure the Duke patted Fred on the back and said "well done". Fred retorted hotly: "If you'd let me ride him the way I wanted, we'd have won."

We had all sorts of people on the staff at Jackdaws, by no means exclusively from the expected backgrounds. Ollie McPhail, for instance, came from Winchester and neither he nor his family knew much about racing. Somehow, he had developed an interest and ridden in a few point-to-points but when he arrived at the yard for his interview he plainly had no idea what his future employer looked like. David Nicholson might have been among the most famous faces in racing but that was lost on Ollie. When he got out of the car with his parents, he walked over to a bare-chested man in shorts and doubtless took him to be the gardener. "I'm looking for David Nicholson," he said boldly. "You've found him," said the Duke. Somehow, he got the job and stayed for years. We did, though, have some who didn't last longer than their first morning. One girl, I remember, tried to get on her horse from the wrong side. Another was legged up and went straight over the other side, landing in an embarrassed heap. When Mark White was head lad he said to one, rather stout new girl: "I can't leg you up, you're too big." She burst into tears and went home, never to be seen again. Mark's view was that if you couldn't take that kind of gentle baiting, there was no future for you in our game.

We all had to put up with our share of humiliations, none more so than a lad called David Cotterell. He had risen to the heights of assistant head lad at Jenny Pitman's yard but when he came to Jackdaws he still had ambitions to be a jockey. Weight was his major impediment and, one Friday morning, he was complaining about how much he needed to lose in order to ride at a local point-to-point the following day. Gordon Clarkson, who never needed any encouragement where pranks were concerned, earnestly told him he had come by a magic potion for losing weight. Once he assured him that A.P.McCoy took the stuff, David was hooked. Gordie went off to his room and came back with a bottle, handed it over to David and told him to take just a single sip. The rest of us knew it was calamine lotion but the victim, desperate for any help in shedding pounds, eagerly swilled back half the bottle. It was midway through second lot when Dave, riding at the front of the string, began to double up in the saddle. He retired to his room, feeling very poorly, and when we went to see him at the end of the morning he was looking quite seriously sick. Somehow, word got back to the Duke, who summoned Gordon to his office and then called a doctor. Dave was living, he assured him, but he might not feel too good for a few hours. The following morning, Dave was well enough to return to work and, though he had prudently given up his afternoon ride, he had lost none of his knack for saying the daftest things. At breakfast time in the canteen, he announced solemnly: "Tell you what, though, that stuff works - I lost 8lb yesterday."

Dave was the type who could make you wonder how on earth he navigated a path through life. Once, he even told us it was his birthday - indeed, insisted his mother had told him that morning it was his birthday - only for it to turn out that he'd got the wrong day. Another time, he almost caused a death on the yard by turning himself into a human torch. It happened because the Duke had discovered ragwort growing wild and knew that it was poisonous to horses. One afternoon, he sent a group of us out to pick it, bag it and drop it back at the yard, where someone was deputised to burn it. There was a lot of the stuff about and the job occupied many summer afternoons. One day, when only a few of us were around, we loaded our catch of ragwort into a Land Rover and took it to the bonfire site. Dave smothered it with petrol but also managed to get plenty on himself and, for good measure, to leave a trail of fuel as he moved away from the stack. When he struck a match, he set himself alight and was in hospital for three days before emerging in a wheelchair with top-to-toe bandaging.

Nicknames, of course, were applied to almost everyone at the yard and Gordon Clarkson was known as 'The Mouth', simply because he always had so much to say. He originated in Northampton and started in racing at John Webber's yard in Banbury, spending a spell in Ireland before ending up at the Duke's. He was good at his job and extremely good at practical jokes, some of them at the expense of the boss himself.

Soon after settling in at Jackdaws, the Duke decided he liked the idea of some apple trees growing in the centre of the yard. A string of young trees were planted, no bigger than twigs, and three years later you could still nearly go over them with a lawnmower. Finally, in the fourth summer, they began to look like proper trees and the

Duke boomed proudly: "One day, we'll have apples on these." Red rag to Gordon. Later the same week, the Duke was off at Ascot and Gordon decreed that he would have his apples. He went to the shops, bought a load of loose apples and some lengths of fine cotton, with which he tied them onto the spindly branches of the still immature trees. Next morning, there was a bit of dew on the ground and it almost looked authentic, but for the little fact that the apples were big and plump and the trees were puny. The Duke marched into the yard to direct operations and his head swivelled at the sight. "Eh, my trees, look at the apples," he said mechanically, briefly taken in by this horticultural miracle. It only took a moment of closer inspection, though, and he was spinning on his heel and shouting "Gordon, you bastard." At times, the Duke could be the easiest person in the world to wind up but, almost without exception, he took it well.

What he did not take well was any of his lads misbehaving in public - and, being the age we were, this was always a possibility. Local point-to-points offered a regular chance for getting out and letting the hair down and I remember one Sunday when a group of us converged on the meeting at Barbury Castle - now home to Alan King and his horses. Ollie, who had been at the yard a fair while by then, had too much to drink - quite a lot too much. With his inhibitions forgotten, he started to show off by shedding his clothes, all of them. The last race had been run and Ollie was in the emptying car park, doing cartwheels in the nude. We've all done daft things but the rest of us sat there open-mouthed at this exhibition until someone suggested we should call a halt to the cabaret. Ollie was enjoying himself by now and it took a posse of us to manhandle him into a car and lock him in until somebody was ready to drive him home.

The Duke knew so many people that there was no chance of an incident like this slipping his attention and, predictably, Ollie was summoned to his office on the Monday morning. He looked dreadful - hangover dreadful - when he went in and he looked shamefaced when he came out, having copped the adult equivalent of six of the best. The Duke had banned him from going to point-to-points and said he had to work every weekend for the next couple of months. As it turned out, he was offered a ride in a point only a couple of weeks later and, throwing himself on the Duke's mercy, was allowed to take it providing he came straight back to the yard afterwards. We went along for the fun and did the gentlemanly thing by letting all his tyres down. That, too, got back to the Duke, and his office was full the next morning, when he started to issue the ritual lecture before bursting into helpless laughter.

I was no angel and I did get the full Nicholson treatment occasionally, but after a while it only really bothered me if it had anything to do with my riding. The good thing about him was that he might yell at you in the morning but he'd still speak to you in the afternoon. Once it was said, it was finished.

Punctuality was my biggest problem, especially once I moved out of the hostel and started sharing a house with my good friend Richard Burton, now a successful point-to-point rider. I just wasn't any good at getting out of bed in the mornings but, somehow, I seemed to get away with it at work more often than not. Richard would cop the flak instead, the Duke shouting at him for not getting me up in time. My ex-housemate remains bewildered by the injustice of it to this day.

Looking back now, I see that I was one of the favoured at Jackdaws. For whatever reason, the Duke took a liking to me and the way I went about things. That was my good fortune, and thankfully remains so, because the man is still a trusted friend and adviser - not to mention amusing social companion at such times as Royal Ascot, where his post-race car park parties are the stuff of legend. I know, however, that a lot of people knock the Duke and I fully understand why. He is a highly opinionated man and those opinions are not easily swayed, even if the rest of the world considers he has got it wrong. If he takes a dislike to you, there is little point in trying to speak to him because you are highly unlikely to win him round. Having this type of black-and-white personality, in addition to one of the highest profiles in racing for a great many years, meant that he was a magnet for publicity, an easy man to write about. And I honestly feel that many did not bother to understand him.

His faults were plain to see. He would upset people, sometimes deliberately, sometimes because he might have had a glass of brandy too many before racing. He did not play the hail-fellow-well-met game very well. He called a spade a shovel. His 'Dukeish' manner, one hand on the breast of his jacket while the other poked the listener in the chest, could be taken as arrogant or rude, and often was. He bullied people, sometimes without even knowing it or meaning to offend. One day at Kempton, he even hit out at a photographer who was hassling a distraught Adrian Maguire after his last-fence fall in the King George VI Chase. After some of my recent experiences with prying cameramen, I have some sympathy with him on that one. The Duke was seldom out of the spotlight, for one reason or another, and of course he thrived on the attention. I think, though, that only those of us who worked under him for a period of years got to know the real man. Some will have emerged disliking him, some left pretty quickly because he scared them, but those who stayed built up more affection and appreciation of the man as time went on. We all got bawled out, we all felt bullied at times, but working at Jackdaws was character-building. I certainly would not have swapped it.

I found him a very easy man to ride for. Maybe I'm the type who tries to get on with people, rather than seeing the bad side - it's certainly true that I haven't fallen out with a trainer for a long time and I never fell out with the Duke. He'd tell me if I'd ridden one badly but that was part of his job. What he would not do was tie you down with elaborate instructions and then rage if you failed to follow them. His riding instructions, in fact, seldom varied. He liked his jockeys to ride a proper race, get upsides the leaders at the second last and win if possible. We had the odd horse like Mysilv, the winner of the Triumph Hurdle for juveniles at the 1994 Cheltenham Festival, who loved to front-run but the Duke was generally happy to have us settled in sixth or seventh and make ground quietly.

If handicap marks worried him, he never let on. Sometimes, I would get carried away on an easy winner, keep pushing to the line and extend the margin to 15 lengths, when I could have done far more to deflect the attentions of the handicapper by easing it right down on the run-in. I know trainers who would slaughter a jockey for this but whenever I came back, usually full of stumbling apologies, the Duke's answer would usually be that there was nothing to worry about because the horse would soon be novice chasing.

Jackdaws was never a big gambling yard. Of course, the lads had a bet now and again if they fancied one, and I'm sure the likes of Alan King and Gordon had their share of stable touches, but the Duke himself never seemed very interested in punting - not unless someone insulted one of his horses and he would back them out of sheer bravado, anyway. His horses were always doing their best, that I do know, and I genuinely believe that goes for the vast majority of the big yards nowadays. Jump racing is highly competitive now and the best means of staying ahead of the game is through volume of winners. Fiddling around with horses' handicap marks until the day when you might have a punt on them is a recipe for failure. It's hard enough to keep National Hunt horses sound, let alone to spirit them into the winners' enclosure on one appointed day.

The Duke would know all this far better than me. After all, by the time I turned up at Jackdaws, he had already spent more than 40 years in racing, 25 of them as a trainer. Top horses such as Broadsword, Very Promising, Charter Party and Waterloo Boy had already been through the yard and, after a long wait to break his Festival duck, Cheltenham winners had been plentiful. The Duke had also endured some bad times, though, when money was a real problem, and I was fortunate to arrive soon after his salvation had been delivered. Colin Smith had been an owner at Condicote for some time but he bought Jackdaws Castle and installed the Duke as his trainer just when his financial fortunes were at their lowest. It led, I think, to the most fulfiling years he was to have as a trainer - not only on the course, where he once again became champion, dethroning Martin Pipe, but in the business of building up a training establishment from nothing. The Duke designed all the facilities at Jackdaws and, for a few years, had things just how he had dreamed they would be. The fact that it worked so well, generating so many winners, showed how well he knew horses and their needs.

The final years, though, were fraught with uncertainty. First, there was the Duke's fall-out with Adrian, who had been such a fine stable jockey and such an inspiration to younger riders like me. I'd like to think David regrets the episode, certainly the shape it took and the impressions that were given, because I don't think Adrian deserved to leave under such a cloud. The fact that I was the direct beneficiary left me with very mixed feelings and, for some time, a sense of embarrassment whenever I met Adrian.

Perhaps, by then, the Duke was already having his problems with Colin Smith. At the time, I did not know our landlord well and I was certainly unsure of the basis for their fall-out. There were plenty of rumours around the yard, as you would expect in such an environment, but the truth was probably hard to detect. Colin frequented the Hollow Bottom pub in Naunton, part-owned by our 'rival' cotswold trainers Nigel Twiston-Davies and Peter Scudamore, and there would generally be some gossip coming from that source after a weekend, which predictably irritated the boss. He, too, was capable of propaganda, though, and with two strong-minded characters involved it is easy to see how what might have begun as a minor disagreement escalated into something that neither could bring himself to solve.

It was terribly sad for the two of them, as they had been the driving forces behind the best new training establishment in the country. They had also enjoyed some terrific times together with Colin's horses, notably Charter Party who won the 1988 Gold Cup. Even while they were on poor terms, Anzum was doing them both proud.

The sadness, though, spread throughout the yard, along with all the anxieties that accompany such a situation. For six months, we all knew that our boss and our landlord were at each other's throats but what we did not know was how it was all going to end. We kept hearing that Colin wanted David out and that he was keen to sell the yard. The Duke, for his part, was digging his feet in, as he would, and insisting to all that he would be there until he decided to leave. Eventually, he achieved a certain dignity by choosing - and announcing - his own retirement, but it was not the way he would have wanted his career to end, nor was it what he deserved.

Personally, selfishly even, I felt bitter about the situation because I'd had a great time at Jackdaws for over six years and I was still riding a lot of good horses for David, who were generally running to their potential. I didn't want him to pack up and I felt sure he was still training as well as ever when he was left to get on with it. Too much of his time, however, was being taken up in a crusade for survival and, eventually, there was only going to be one winner. David called me into the office one day, late in 1999, and told me that Alan King would be taking over the licence. In a sense, the Duke had manipulated the situation as he wished, leaving Alan with the yard. As we now know, though, it was a purely temporary arrangement and even when Colin installed his own man, in Richard Phillips, it lasted barely a year before the place was sold. I wonder whether Colin Smith is sad, on reflection, that it came to this. His disillusionment must have been strong, and possibly he didn't have the heart to continue running Jackdaws as a business after the very public split with the Duke. The fact that he identified the site and had the inspiration for the yard, though, must surely mean something and I hope the good memories outweigh the bad. Certainly, Jonjo O'Neill - installed by the new owner J.P.McManus - is busily showing what a fantastic place it is to train winners. I've never been anywhere that rivals Jackdaws and it definitely has the best National Hunt gallops in the country. Glancing up at the place, when I go in the Plough for a drink on Saturday evenings, I can't help feeling just a little sad.

For a time, after his retirement, the Duke was a lost soul. I'm sure he was hurt by what had happened, though he would be too proud to show it, and despite being past his 60th birthday he was not ready for a quiet life at their new home in a cotswold village. Dinah, his wife, is a marvel in the garden but I could never see David settling for such relaxing pursuits. He loved to be involved in things, to have a say in their running. Preferably, of course, he wanted a job in racing but the problem was that he was over-qualified for most of the positions that were on offer and it was hard for him to find anything satisfying. He had a short spell as racing manager for Stan Clarke but it is great that he has now landed a more suitable position, with the British Horseracing Board putting him in charge of promoting British breeding. It is an area he knows plenty about and he is already doing the job with great enthusiasm. It's ideal for him, because he knows everyone, it allows him to go racing with a purpose and even gives him a reason to socialise. I'm glad he has got something to get him up in the morning, something to concentrate his very active mind. Indirectly, it has also helped heal the wounds with Colin Smith, whose Crandon Park Stud sponsors the mares' final each year. They have a neutral subject to talk about now, which has to be good. Life is too short to bear grudges.

Just because we are no longer trainer and stable jockey does not mean we have lost contact. The Duke would never allow that, and I would not want it. He generally phones me two or three times a week and loves to know what is going on - the gossip and rumour of the weighing-room are still his stock in trade. He will occasionally ring, too, if he thinks I got beaten in a race I might have won, though usually he raises the subject gently and is far more encouraging than corrective. "If he wasn't good enough, he couldn't win", he will boom, and somehow it still makes me feel better. Sometimes.

I have met nobody else like David Nicholson in racing and I doubt if I ever shall. The sport is full of characters, some more shallow than others, but if there is a man who inspires such high emotions, such loyalty on the one hand and dislike on another, such a vast array of anecdotes - all of them true, I shall be very surprised. I have a lot to thank him for and the best thing, from my viewpoint, is that my first Cheltenham Festival winner, on Anzum, was also his last. I can think of no more fitting way to remember him than that.

Rusty Bridge

4.
A Family Affair
R u s t y   B r i d g e

In reviewing the horses that have been important to me, where else could I start but here? Dear old Rusty Bridge did the family proud for years on end and it was he - with a little help from the human Johnsons - who kickstarted my riding career. Rusty gave me my first public ride, my first winner under Rules and an early education in how hard jockeys need to work to get the best out of horses. And it all meant so very much more for being our own cottage industry - bred, owned, trained and ridden by the Johnson family.

I was sixteen and Rusty was seven when we first linked up in a race. It was the Larkhill point-to-point and it took place on January 27th, 1994. The date, rather than the year, is imprinted on my mind like an unforgettable telephone number because it was on that day that the new point-to-point season began and I had mentally marked it off for months beforehand as the day on which I intended to make my debut. It didn't matter that Larkhill, down in Wiltshire, was far from being a local meeting for us, it was the fact that it was the opening fixture that counted. I couldn't wait any longer. The family was fully alerted to this and, I think, privately quite happy to go along with the sense of anticipation.

I'd been working at Jackdaws Castle for six months by then and things were happening a bit slowly for my liking. It wasn't that the novelty had worn off (I don't think that has happened, even now) or that I suddenly considered myself worthy of getting on the Duke's horses ahead of Adrian Maguire. I was a bit more grounded than that but I still felt anxious to make a start and the one person I knew who was likely to give me that first ride was my grandfather. Fortunately, he had just the horse for the job.

Our dynasty of horses, begun by Bridge Ash and named after a house on the family farm, have tended to share similar characteristics - they stay all day and do nothing very fast. It makes them the ideal horses for a young jockey to be trained up on, and Rusty was no exception. He was the first foal out of Bridge Ash, sired by an unfashionable stallion named Rustingo. The stud fee was a mere £50, so a Cheltenham winner was not expected. As it turned out, though, Rusty (who could have had that name for his rust colour rather than his breeding) did eventually win a race at jumping's headquarters, albeit in a hunter chase.

He had already won two point-to-points by the time I badgered Grandad into letting me ride him at Larkhill, so he had to be entered for the Men's Open race (usually the most competitive on any pointing card) and, unfortunately, he was obliged to carry 12st 7lb. On the advice of the Duke, I had been to see Tom Buckingham, one of the southern valets, a fortnight before the race, and he had told me, reassuringly, that I would be turned out looking like a jockey even if I couldn't ride like one. I left armed with this dubious vote of confidence, along with such accessories as a weight-cloth, which was to come in rather handy. I weighed 8st 7lb stripped so I carried a giant, borrowed saddle and a massive load of lead. The poor horse must have used up some of his energy lumping 4st around the parade ring.

Mum and Dad had travelled down with me, of course, and stood in the little paddock as Grandad gave his instructions. They were not complicated and equated to jumping off in front and staying there as long as possible. He always did like his horses ridden handy and, with Rusty, there was really no point in approaching a race any other way. He was very slow but he had stamina to burn and would still be galloping, at his own, single speed, when many of the others had had enough. In time, I was to wish there were some five mile races, because that would really have brought him into his own, but at Larkhill that day, three miles was quite far enough for me.

I couldn't get him to the front at any stage but I pushed and scrubbed for all I was worth, urging him to go half a stride quicker than he was physically able. Fortunately, he was a very safe ride (only Warren Marston ever fell off him, a fact I have reminded him of more than once) and he skillfully put himself right at the fences even if my manic pushing had got him on a bad stride. For a time, inside the last mile, I thought we were going to finish fourth, which would have made my day as it merited a place in the homespun winners' enclosure. It was not to be, though. We were beaten a length for fourth and I had to dismount in the field alongside, not the same thrill at all. By that stage, in all honesty, I was almost too tired to be registering anything around me. I had to stand still for a minute to get my breath back, then gingerly slid the saddle and its four-stone burden off his back and into my wilting arms. Dad offered to help but no, this was my ride and I had to do everything myself, so with a martyred pride I staggered back to weigh in, a jockey of sorts at last.

He became my regular ride after that. Grandad had always been pleased that I wanted to be a jockey, so there was plenty of encouragement from that direction, but I told him firmly that I was going to ride the horse, anyway. It's amazing how headstrong a 16-year-old can be when he has a goal in his sights. Every ride on Rusty was the same in certain respects. I'd be pushing and slapping him before we jumped the first, anxious to prevent him losing touch in the early stages of the race. Without fail, he would respond willingly, or as willingly as his natural lack of speed allowed.

My first pointing winner, achieved a month or so after that initial ride, was a rare 'outside booking', Space Mariner for a local farmer called Tom Bailey, but the great day of that season was the final Saturday of April, when Rusty won at 25-1 to give me my first success at a regulation meeting. If I could have written the script myself, I would not have changed a thing, for not only was it achieved on the family horse, it also came at our local track, Hereford, and in a race quite spookily titled: The Next Generation Hunter Chase. It was almost as if the race planners had known the result in advance.

The starting price is enough to indicate that Rusty was not exactly a hot fancy that day but, in hindsight, conditions were pretty much ideal - an extended three-miles trip on quick ground against opponents who were generally no quicker than he was. The blot on the race looked to be a horse called Brown Windsor, who had won plenty of decent races for Nicky Henderson and, in his previous outing, had finished second in the Aintree Foxhunters. He was sent off as the 7-4 favourite but was pulled-up when well beaten and it could be that jumping those Aintree fences had left a mental mark on him. Rusty had been through no such ordeal and, though he was predictably flat out from the start, I managed to keep him in front all the way and we jumped the last fence four or five lengths clear. I gave him two right-handed cracks as we landed but I was then either too tired, too inexperienced or a combination of both to pull my stick through into my left hand and keep him straight. The result was that he drifted from the inside running rail right across the chase and hurdles courses, giving away lengths in the process. We crossed the line right in front of the stands, while The Malakarma, our nearest pursuer, had kept a more conventional line to the post. It went to a photo and there was an agonising wait before we were declared the winners by a head.

A lot of my friends were around, quite apart from most of the family, and in hindsight it doesn't get much better than that. When you are 16, I think you just bulldoze through life imagining that such doors will be opened for you and it is only recently, reflecting on the day, that I appreciate quite what an emotional thrill it was. At the time, it flashed past in a haze of triumph and vindication.

Two days later, Monday morning at Jackdaws Castle, David Nicholson marched across to address me. "Well done," he said gruffly. "But from now on, you ride out with a stick in your left hand every day." I'm not sure if he had been at Hereford on the day but he had bothered to watch the race and, rather than feeling deflated, I was just pleased he was taking an interest. All the more pleased later that day, though, for it was the May Bank Holiday and I had picked up another point-to-point ride. When that won, too, I began to think this racing was a very simple game.

I rode Rusty in four more hunter chases before the end of that season but he didn't register another win. He was a gallant second, back at Hereford two weeks after his victory, and the following week we took him to Cheltenham for the feature race on the annual

May hunter-chase card. It was my first ride on the course and, although Rusty had no chance against Teaplanter, who had finished second in the Cheltenham Foxhunters that year, he ran another game race to be runner-up.

The Johnsons plainly did not believe in giving their horse an easy time, because he had 15 runs the following season and it was not until the 13th of them that he got his head in front. It was May of 1995 and the first race of a Friday evening card at Stratford. Being a tight circuit, quite unsuited to staying types, Rusty would normally have been severely disadvantaged at Stratford but this was a particular type of race, its runners restricted by the stipulation that the owners and jockeys had to be related. This was all too tempting for us and, of course, it eliminated most of the quality hunter-chasing opposition, but there was one horse declared that I felt we couldn't beat. Sandybraes was trained by David Nicholson and I had won twice on him that season - at Market Rasen, where I got plenty of publicity despite nearly falling off him at the last, and back at Stratford the previous month. Since then, though, he had been sold to the Hutsby family with the express purpose of letting Fred, newly arrived at Jackdaws Castle, get some riding experience. This was doubly bad news for me. I'd been looking forward to picking up another winner or two on a horse I had come to regard as my ride, and now it looked as if he might deprive Rusty of another family triumph. I had reckoned without Fred's innocence on horseback, though. I jumped the first okay on Rusty and was still just in front at the second. Out of the corner of my eye, I caught sight of Sandybraes, and of Fred taking a star jump out the side door. I was genuinely upset for him, because he was and is a top bloke, but as clear second favourite I knew we now had a decent chance. Rusty did not make it easy for me, dropping to the rear of the seven remaining runners at halfway, but I drove him back into the lead at the last and he won going away.

Cheltenham's hunter-chase meeting was switched to Warwick that year due to drainage work at Prestbury Park - a particular shame for me, as Rusty won the four-miler, initiating a double I would dearly like to have registered at Cheltenham. Still, though I refused to believe it on the day, there was time enough for that.

Rusty went on for a few years more, even running in some open handicap chases one year, but he was never going to be better than hunting class. He was put down after suffering an injury on Mum's gallops and I remember it left me with a lump in the throat. Whatever else happens during my career, I shall certainly never forget him.

His half-brother, Derring Bridge, also came on the scene while I was still an amateur. Though he was a similar, staying type, he had a good bit more class - but, being by that quirky old hurdler Derring Rose, he was also a monkey. In March of 1995, I won a novice hurdle on him at Ludlow but he didn't win again until June of the following year at Southwell. He's still around now and won his 14th race (eight over hurdles and six chases) in the late summer of 2001. At rising 13, retirement is beckoning now but if Rusty set me on the right road, 'Herbie' ensured I stayed there. I think I have won on him ten times and I was mighty peeved to miss an 11th through suspension. I went away for a few days and came back eager to know from Mum how he had run. I was pleased for her when she said he'd won, just sorry to have let the ride winner into other hands. "And who rode him?" I asked innocently. A.P.McCoy was the answer. Story of my life.

Milton Bradley

5.
A rural education
M i l t o n   B r a d l e y

It turned out that he was virtually a family friend, a fellow farmer my father and grandad had known for years through many days together at West Country markets, but I got to know Milton Bradley through the Turf telephone directory. His was one of many numbers I jotted down in the search for rides in amateur races and it was my good fortune, in this largely unrewarding process, that J.M.Bradley was among the few trainers to respond positively and give the raw and unknown Mr R.Johnson, claiming 7lb, a chance.

I was in my first summer at Jackdaws Castle and had the illogical impatience that only a teenager can know. A few point-to-point winners had provided all the convincing I needed and nothing, in my mind, could now stop me being a jockey. Nothing, that is, bar the small problem of finding someone to give me a ride. David Nicholson, gruff but encouraging, suggested I should not waste the summer months but try and get some valuable riding experience on the flat. There were plenty of races restricted to amateur riders, he told me, and I should put my name around, make myself available. He added, very kindly, that I could use the office telephone to ring round after evening stables and I took him at his word. I don't suppose he realised the bill he was letting himself in for.

Every time an amateur riders' race cropped up among the five-day cards in the *Racing Post*, I would take the paper into the office after work, drag out the directory and ring every trainer with an entry. It didn't matter if there were 25 different trainers on the list, I would ring them all. There were many times through that summer when I spent all evening in there, dialling and then redialling numbers, intent on tracking down trainers and permit holders who would probably rather have been doing anything but chat to an eager 17-year-old with big ideas. I suspect I got one ride from every 100 calls and it could be a deflating business, though the fact that I never got completely demoralised says a lot about how much I wanted that single ride. Looking back, the effort I expended was beneficial in two ways, teaching me how very hard it is for a young jockey to get going and refining a telephone technique that started out extremely tongue-tied.

The third benefit was that it introduced me to Mr Bradley. Milton was always on my list and would often have several entries in a race, most of them so lowly rated that the majority of amateur riders were unable to make the weight. As I could ride comfortably at 9st 7lb I had a big advantage. I don't think I ever got to speak to Milton himself during these long evenings - it was always his wife, Ruth, who answered the phone. Usually, she would be very friendly, taking my number and promising to speak to her husband about his plans and then ring me back. I heard this kind of thing from a lot of yards but, unlike most, Mrs Bradley did not let me down. She always did ring back and, one day, she said I could ride one for them. It was the start of a relationship that taught me a great deal about the different levels and demands of training, quite apart from giving me that precious education in flat race-riding.

It was the mid-1990s and Milton, who had trained jumpers for more than 30 years from his lovely old farm near Chepstow, had only recently diversified into the flat. Typical of the man, as I was to find out, he did not wait around to run them all at his local meetings but dispatched them far and wide. The one winner I was to ride for him on the flat did, by chance, come at Chepstow, over seven furlongs, but he booked me for rides at courses so remote I had to look some of them up on the map. Frequently, I would phone Mum and ask if she fancied going racing with me the next day. Only when she had agreed would I tell her that the meeting was at Hamilton, or maybe Beverley.

Milton would always be there himself, which impressed me even more when I learned he habitually drove the horsebox to these far-flung venues, then saddled and led up his runners himself. Even at this stage, watching him operate was an education to me in how hard some trainers have to graft to get by. But there was a lot more learning to be done when he asked me down to Meads Farm to school some of his jumpers. Most of the Bradley string were extremely cheap sales horses and, inevitably, there were some disaffected creatures among them. Milton had a theory that a horse gone sour on the flat should be tried first over hurdles and then over fences - if it was still no good, he would get rid of it. This meant we had some interesting types to school, though to his great credit he had loose-schooled them all himself first and I never rode anything there that I considered unsafe.

Milton's method of schooling owed something to the French, I suppose, in its intensity if not its sophistication. He had two fences, that he had made himself, out in a farm field and we would simply go up and down, round and round, until the horses were fluent.

Only then would we repair to the farmhouse kitchen for breakfast, which Mrs Bradley had somehow managed to cook in between doing what most stables would consider the work of three people.

She is a quite fantastic woman and just to list all her jobs would make most people tired. She cooks all the lads' food, helps to run the farm, takes the calls for the skip-hire business they run as a sideline and keeps the accounts up to date. Then comes the serious stuff. Ruth enters and declares all the horses and answers every phone call from owners and would-be riders. During breakfast, the one line in the house seemed to ring every 30 seconds. As Milton sat down with his tea, she would present him with a list of entries and a second list of potential jockeys. Without ceremony, he would go through the riders, striking them off one by one, mostly rejecting them because, in one of his favourite phrases, 'he never does what he's told'.

Being at an age, and of an upbringing, to speak only when spoken to, I sat and absorbed the lesson here. Milton's pet hate is disobedient jockeys. While I was riding for him (and I have no reason to think he has changed), he never complained about how his horse had run, even if it had finished tailed-off, so long as I had followed instructions. "It's harder to get them ridden right than it is to train them," he would say. And it was not just idle talk. A champion jockey would be treated just the same as a 7lb claimer - if he did his own thing, rather than what the trainer told him, he would not ride for the stable again. In time, when I began to ride some hurdlers for the yard, Milton's instructions would be simple and unvarying. "Bounce him out sharply," he would say, "stay on the inner, don't give any ground away and do your best." It was not rocket science and, being anxious to please, I tried to follow his orders slavishly. Sometimes, the horse was just not up to the job and would quickly be out of contention but Milton never minded that, so long as I had done his bidding. It taught me that orders are important and that the trainer is the man in charge.

I learned a whole lot more than that from Milton Bradley, though. I learned that attitude and atmosphere could mean more than mere facilities. I had been spoiled at Jackdaws, where the horses and amenities were just about as good as money could buy. Milton's yard at Sedbury could hardly have presented a bigger contrast. The lads had to do more horses and work longer hours, yet they were loyal, diligent and obviously happy. The lead was given by Milton, Ruth and their family (two daughters and a son), all of whom grafted selflessly to make the operation work, yet plainly got so much pleasure out of it that you hardly ever heard a complaint.

It was good for me to see how hard some trainers have to work, and how success can come from fairly unpromising material. Milton is a very modest man and he buys essentially modest horses, usually for a relative pittance. He bridles at the very idea of paying £20,000 and evidently has a terrific eye for picking out bargains at the sales. Often, he has picked up horses that have lost their form in another yard and revitalised them with his own brand of care and attention. He told me he hates having vets around the place and prefers the natural remedies of 'Doctor Green' - grass and rest - for sick horses. These can be dismissed as the rustic theories of a countryman, especially when you know Milton used to milk 110 cows a day single-handed and started his racing life on the outlawed 'flapping' tracks of South Wales, but the results he has produced of late cut short any such cynicism.

He is in his late sixties now, an age when most of us would want to put our feet up and watch others do the work, but, far from considering retirement, he is having the time of his life. In the flat seasons of 2000 and 2001 he trained 47 and 62 winners respectively, running up impressive individual tallies with battle-hardened sprinters like Juwwi and Brevity, who would often run twice a week with no ill effects.

People like Milton and David Evans, another trainer who maximises his resources through sheer hard work, are easily knocked by the sophisticats of the flat but they meet a particular market and do it wonderfully well. In all the times I went down to Sedbury, I never once saw a horse in the yard that looked anything other than fit and happy, no matter how often they had run. Milton was short-listed as flat trainer of the year last season and if I'd been allowed a vote he would certainly have got it.

A couple of years ago, one breakfast-time after a schooling session, Milton told me that he would never buy a jumps-bred horse again. After so many years of concentrating on the National Hunt side - and it remains his love - he had concluded that it just didn't work for a yard of his type. The horses were becoming expensive, they were prone to going wrong and he could not run them nearly as often as those on the flat. In his gentle way, he was telling me there was no point my coming down regularly any more, because there just wouldn't be any rides for me. Though I understood his thinking - how could you argue with it when you see what he has achieved lately? - it was a sad day for me.

Milton gave me a start when others were reluctant. The fortune we shared with a fabulous little chestnut called Maggotts Green is dealt with in the next chapter, but it was not so much the winners that made me so grateful but the whole Bradley experience. It is a cosy, tumbledown, farmyard set-up but it taught me that state-of-the-art facilities alone do not guarantee that horses will win regularly. It's the person who trains them and keeps them happy that is most important.

Maggotts Green

6.
The first breakthrough
M a g g o t t s   G r e e n

Imagine this: you are just 19, setting out on your first full season as a fully-fledged professional jockey with none of the weight allowances that benefit aspirant riders in the conditional system. You need a good start, need to be noticed, and you are given the ride on a horse that seems able to run at least once a week and is generally better than the fast-ground opposition she encounters on the summer jumping circuit. Maggotts Green, a chestnut mare trained on the welsh borders by Milton Bradley, was that horse and she made the transition into the top sphere so much easier for me than it might have been.

It was the summer of 1996. Under the guidance of Dave Roberts and David Nicholson, I had left the amateur ranks midway through the previous season and become a professional. Things went well and I rode enough winners to lose my weight allowance quicker than most. It is at this point that many young jockeys find it a struggle, because trainers can no longer 'poach' the advantage of taking a few pounds off a horse and are thus less inclined to use youth over experience. You need a few breaks then and mine came in the form of Maggotts Green.

We actually went back quite a long way. Two years earlier, in October 1994, I had won an amateurs' chase on her at Ludlow. It was during that summer that I'd spent endless evening hours on the phone in the Jackdaws Castle office, seeking rides in amateur flat races and finding that Mr Bradley, and his ever charming wife, was one of my best sources. I suppose I can't have done much to upset him on the flat as the booking came through to take my first ride over jumps for the yard. It was a welcome boost, too. After all the excitement with Rusty Bridge the previous season, I'd made a slow start to the new term. It was predictable, of course, but that did not stop me getting impatient. I remember being pumped up with excitement over breakfast at Jackdaws on the morning of the Ludlow race, because the papers had him down as second or third favourite. These days, if I don't go to a meeting riding a couple of short-priced horses I begin to worry that something has gone wrong, but times change. One ride with a chance was a very big day for me at 17.

The ground was firm, there were only five runners and Maggotts Green was able to dominate, as Milton liked her to do. Coming to the last, I still felt we needed a good jump to repel Parson's Way, the nearest challenger, and I recall taking my whip hand off the reins and giving her a smack as she took off. This was not a manoeuvre I had attempted in a race before and it was done more in instinctive hope than confident command. It worked, though, and she flew the fence and strode away to win by 12 lengths.

She was a seven-year-old then and, although clearly never going to be a superstar, she travelled well through her races and was an absolute christian to ride. She had a big white blaze on her nose and was a real flashy individual but there was no showing off at the obstacles - if I got into trouble, she would get me out of it.

Until the Ludlow race, she had generally been ridden by Rodney Farrant and he was back on her next time out, in an open handicap. Typical of Milton, who never believed in leaving his horses in their stables for long, it was a mere three days later, at Hereford, and my disappointment at losing the ride was partly assuaged when she could finish only third, despite being sent off favourite.

It was to be almost two years before Maggotts Green saw the winners' enclosure again. The following season she ran 11 times without scoring - the closest she came was when we were reunited in the corresponding amateurs' race at Ludlow, where she narrowly failed to repeat the performance and lost out by a length to a useful horse called Mr Entertainer. Milton campaigned Maggotts through the winter that year, sometimes in quite decent company and on easier ground than she really liked. The outcome was that she dropped down the handicap and started the next season on a very favourable mark. That, and the fast ground she adored, set her up for an amazingly busy and productive late summer campaign.

In a shade over seven weeks, Milton ran her nine times. She won five, was second once and third on the other three occasions. Sure, they weren't great races and often the prize money was poor but she collected more than £20,000 for her owner, Mr Hayward, and must have given him a tremendous amount of fun.

Of those nine races, I rode her seven times and the one downside to this story is that she won - for Tony McCoy and Timmy Murphy - both times I missed out. My three wins on her came in a 25-day spell when she won four races in succession and created quite a little fan club on the Midlands circuit. The sequence began at Southwell on August 13, then took in Hereford eight days later before she won for Timmy at Newton Abbot on Bank Holiday Monday (I was hardly in a position to complain as, meanwhile, I was sampling the unique flavour of Cartmel for the first time and coming away with a treble).

Thankfully, Milton is a loyal man and as I was available again the following Saturday he put me back on the mare at Stratford. To be honest, I didn't go there feeling confident, partly due to the fact that the run of success had sent her soaring up the weights but also because this was a three-mile race and she had never won over that far. The opposition was hotter, too, with Gordon Richards sending a well-regarded horse called Early Morning Light down from Cumbria. All things considered, I was not surprised that Maggotts was sent off at 9-1, almost the outsider of the six-strong field. Neither, knowing the man as I had come to do, was I surprised when Milton's previous race instructions did not vary at all from his customary mantra. There was no question of concern over her getting the trip or efforts to hold her up and conserve energy - go out and be positive on her was the message. So I did. She needed some stoking up in the last mile, and there were a few strides when I thought she might not stay the trip, but she had tremendous heart and simply kept on battling, winning by a length and a quarter and, remarkably, breaking the three-mile course record in the process.

The winning run was over but the mare was kept busy and never let anyone down. A week after her Stratford run she was out again at Worcester, finishing second behind Tartan Tradewinds in a grade of race to which she had never previously aspired. Soon, now, the summer ground was going to ease and the good horses would be out, making life distinctly different, but Milton went to the well once more, the following Saturday at Market Rasen, and my determination to keep the partnership intact meant that I rode her with a broken thumb.

The coincidence was remarkable, for it involved the other horse that had contributed generously to my early fortunes that year, Stately Home. He had only managed a selling hurdle win the previous season yet now, invigorated by his trainer Peter Bowen, he had won six firm-ground chases on the bounce - and I had ridden him in five of them. His run, too, had come to an end and the previous day, at Huntingdon, perhaps showing the signs of his busy campaign, he had jumped sloppily before unseating me three out. I jarred my thumb as I landed but the dent to my pride hurt more. I had no further rides that afternoon and I convinced myself that it was only bruised and set off, next morning, to keep my appointment with Maggotts Green at Market Rasen.

Halfway through the race, I knew for certain that the thumb was broken. It was agony if anything even touched my hand, so I simply took it out of service and literally rode the rest of the race with my reins and stick in one hand and the other trailing uselessly by my side. She was such a safe conveyance that I trusted her even to carry me round riding one-handed, and sure enough she completed without alarms. She only finished third, though, and I just have to reassure myself that she could not have won, even with a two-handed jockey.

It was a golden time in my career, Stately Home and Maggotts Green giving me the sort of run that most teenagers could only dream of. Maggotts somehow meant the most, though, because she had swept me round in that amateurs' race at Ludlow two years earlier, just when I was wondering where my next winner might come from.

Milton, who has an enviably cheerful attitude to racing and is just as happy winning a seller as a valuable conditions event, got some publicity out of the sequence of wins and, inevitably, some of the glory was reflected in my direction. It was the perfect start to a season in which I was to ride 100 winners for the first time and rise rapidly in profile. Pretty soon, I was riding horses of a far higher class than Maggotts Green, yet she had been influential in getting me to that level and giving people confidence in my ability to ride over fences.

I've seen plenty of examples of talented young riders, either amateur or conditional, who struggle to make progress despite riding a lot of winners in the races we call 'bumpers' - flat races for National Hunt horses and jockeys.

Doing well in that sphere can, oddly enough, count against you as trainers unwittingly categorise riders on what they have achieved. Rob Massie, a good friend of mine at David Nicholson's yard, was a prime sufferer in this regard. He was actually a very decent rider over fences but he probably had no more than 20 steeplechase rides in four or five years. His problem was that he rode so many bumper winners that everyone earmarked him for that sort of race - and bumpers tend to be an afterthought on a card, the race that will never get much exposure. Rob rode out his claim almost unnoticed and found that no trainers wanted to trust him riding over fences because their memory told them he was just a bumper jockey. Finally, thoroughly frustrated by his lack of advancement, Rob uprooted and went to America, where he is doing extremely well - even in the timber races that require a high level of jumping ability. I'm glad he is happy and successful in his new home but, if things had worked out differently - if he, not I, had picked up the ride on Maggotts Green - the roles might have been reversed.

Dave Roberts

7.
A very special agent
D a v e   R o b e r t s

The question I am asked more than any other is why I have the same agent as Tony McCoy - the same, indeed, as the great majority of my main rivals. I am not surprised at the public bewilderment. It must seem like Sir Alex Ferguson continuing to manage Manchester United but then taking on Arsenal and Liverpool as well. Nobody, of course would be capable of such an undertaking, not just in terms of workload but in equitable division of time and attention. The players would rebel. Yet Dave Roberts somehow does it for the jump jockeys, and with such efficiency and integrity that, for each of us that employ him to book our rides, there is no more important man in our working lives.

At last count, Dave was handling 18 jockeys and if most of us are in the top division then, to degrees, he has been responsible. His aim each year now is to put his jockeys on more than 1,000 winners and he meets the target unerringly. It is scarcely an exaggeration to say that he has changed the way racing operates, because it is not just the top jockeys who depend upon him but many of the top trainers, too. Dave knows better than anyone which horses are likely to run in which races and he contrives to make this knowledge helpful to all without, apparently, upsetting anyone. It is an awesome act of conjuring.

Dave is in his early 40's and works out of his own home in Redhill, Surrey. I have never been there and I don't know of any jockey who has. Unlike a lot of agents, Dave has neither ridden nor trained horses and he hardly ever goes racing. If these sound negative recommendations, think again, because one of his great strengths is being able to watch every race on TV in his office, analyse and memorise the performance of individual horses and make use of it to the benefit of his jockeys. He may not be a horse person but he is a very good judge of racing, which is all that matters.

So highly is he regarded by the jockeys' profession that there is heated competition to get on his books. A couple of years back, he rejected 22 applicants to join his 'team'. Last year, he told me, it was closer to 50. To be taken on by Dave Roberts is a sign, acknowledged by everyone in racing, that you are thought to be going places. As a badge of honour, they do not come much more prestigious. He does not seek extra business now and tends to take on someone new only when he loses a jockey, probably to retirement. I can imagine the queue already forming for the vacancy that Richard Guest, his first client, will create when he packs up in 2003 but even when Dave has decided on someone suitably promising he will always consult his existing jockeys first. It is unlikely ever to come to it but, theoretically, we could blackball somebody.

These days, he is spoken of with a certain awe within racing but even the country boy who started out at Jackdaws Castle in 1994 had heard of Dave Roberts. He had just piloted Adrian Maguire's thrilling pursuit of Richard Dunwoody in one of the great jockeys' title races of them all. Suddenly, everyone wanted to know Roberts but I did not expect him to want to know me. It was at the start of my second season, after I had ridden half-a-dozen winners fairly quickly, that 'The Duke' called me in and said it was time I had an agent. I had already been phoned by a few characters I had never heard of (nor, significantly, have heard of since) asking if they could take over my rides but the boss said I should leave the matter with him. I was happy to do so and thought nothing more of it - at that age, such things seem sublimely unimportant. It was a fortnight later that he told me Dave Roberts would be doing my rides for the rest of that season, 'to see how things worked out'. I did not know at the time that Dave and the guv'nor had agreed, between them, that I should remain an amateur for the time being, no matter how impatient I became. It is a tactic Dave has encouraged with all the young jockeys he has taken on since, and judging from my experience it has a lot of merit. Dave could doubtless book the boys more rides, and make more instant money from them, if they turned professional sooner but it is a measure of the man that he thinks of the long-term benefits above any short-term profits.

Through all that season and half the next (in which, thankfully, he was happy to keep me on) I knew Dave only by his voice on the phone. I had no idea what he looked like, yet his voice had become so familiar he might have been one of the family. He was like a best friend I had never met, yet I never really thought about this curious aspect of the relationship until one evening when Dave told me he was coming to the races at Towcester the following afternoon and would come and find me 'to introduce myself'. It was only then that I began to wonder how I would recognise him. When the moment came, I didn't. I had weighed out for a ride and was standing in the cluttered lobby of the Towcester weighing-room waiting to hand over the saddle to the trainer. My mind was doubtless elsewhere and when a complete stranger came up and said hello, not even the voice alerted me to who it was. "I'm Dave Roberts," he said finally, which made me feel a shade foolish as I had been speaking to him every day for the previous year and a half. I'm not sure quite what I expected but Dave did look younger than I had imagined any man with his workload could look.

Even now, six years on, I have only met Dave eight or nine times. He usually comes to the Lesters, the jockeys' big celebration night in April, and I've had the odd game of golf with him during the summer. It was after a round in Lambourn that some of the jockeys went on with Dave to the Queen's Arms, a real racing pub in the neighbouring village of East Garston. Dave had arranged to meet Brian Crowley for a chat and duly saw him in the pub, where they shared a chat and a drink. As Brian was leaving, he turned to Tony McCoy and asked if he knew what Dave Roberts looked like, because he had been due to see him there. A.P., puzzled and then amused, broke it to him that he had been chatting with this remarkably anonymous agent for the past 20 minutes.

When we first spoke about arrangements, Dave suggested I should ring him once a day and that is how it has gone on ever since. I avoid the mid-morning period, which I imagine must be his most manic, but I might ring at midday to check on plans for the next day. Despite the pressures of the job, which I'm told he conducts by juggling four separate phones running up an annual bill of more than £10,000, I don't think I have heard him sound even vaguely flustered more than once. He is always contactable other than on Sunday afternoons, when he sometimes switches off his mobile to take his kids to watch Chelsea, one part of his life I will never understand.

I know of agents who ring their jockeys four or five times a day and I've never been able to work out why. Dave is very businesslike and will phone me only if there is a point to it - usually to revise some bookings or direct me to a different meeting but just occasionally to warn me against being too cavalier and risking needless injury. Sometimes he will be on to say that a certain trainer is keen I should ride a novice chaser and might approach me direct.

His point will usually be that it is a horse I should stay well clear of, directing the trainer back to him. Equally, he has rung me when I've been on the way to racing, telling me that one or other jockey has cried off and that I should not under any circumstances take the spare ride in the first. An agent with his laser-like memory for the form and idiosyncrasies of horses can sometimes be as valuable in telling you what not to ride as he is in putting you on winners.

In the early days, when I rang, he would often say there was nothing for me but, looking back, the rides quickly began to accumulate and that was largely down to Dave's unrivalled network of contacts. His methods are quite brilliant and it will come as a surprise to many that he does all his work by hand, neither trusting nor understanding the computer that apparently sits in the corner of his office for the exclusive use of his children.

His day starts unfailingly at 5.30am and can continue until well into the evening. He works with handwritten lists, coloured pens and a calm but meticulous manner that seems to soothe irascible trainers as much as it must surely impress them. I've been in trainers' offices at breakfast time when Dave has rung to leave a message and I've been amused to hear him, other phones audibly chasing him yet still measured and non-committal as he says: 'Dave Roberts here. Just ringing about the handicap chase at Exeter on Thursday. I've got Mick Fitzgerald, Johnny Kavanagh, Richard

Johnson, Norman Williamson and Tony McCoy available. Get back to me if you can.' In his delivery, he has not tried to press the claims of any particular rider, simply offered the choice - that is his gift and that is why he keeps us all happy. As for the listening trainer, he might even feel quite smug at being offered the pick of so many leading jockeys for his runner. It works both ways.

The perks for the trainers do not end there. Dave will ring a lot of them on a daily basis to discuss their plans and requirements and because he is constantly gathering information, he will know the likely runners in any given race before they do. He is also able to judge whether the weights are likely to go up in the handicap races, which is priceless knowledge for a trainer who has an entry a few pounds out of the handicap at the five-day stage. The trainer will then know he can declare the horse and he will not be carrying more weight than he should, while Dave benefits by booking one of his jockeys for the ride.

It is a system that shows how completely Dave is trusted with information by trainers, because to the best of my knowledge he has not fallen out with any of them, despite the delicacy of the information he is handling every day. If he ever needed a new career, heaven forbid, he would make a brilliant public relations officer. He has a deadpan delivery that gives absolutely nothing away and I certainly would not like to play poker against him, but his manner also inspires confidence. I feel I could say anything to him about a horse or a trainer, no matter how uncomplimentary, without the slightest fear that it might be passed on.

He sees things from a different angle to those of us who are at racing every day and that, too, can be valuable. If, for instance, I pick up a ban that I consider harsh I will often ask for his opinion, knowing he will have studied the race and the incident. He is honest enough to tell me if I'm deluding myself but if he does say I am hard done-by, I will know it is worth challenging the decision.

A good agent takes a lot of the strain away from his jockeys. Trainers and owners know there is little point in approaching me direct about riding arrangements because I will always refer them to Dave, who knows far more than I do about where I will be going on any given day and what horses I would be best employed by riding. Ask me on a midwinter Wednesday which of four Saturday meetings I will be riding at and I won't have a clue. I happily leave it to Dave to decide where I am most likely to ride winners and to do all the necessary negotiating with the trainers. He has never let me down yet. These days, Philip Hobbs is my main supplier of rides and winners but I am not retained and there are times when it is obviously advantageous to ride something for my other regular trainers such as Henry Daly and Richard Phillips. Clashes inevitably occur but Dave is adept at working the trainers around to their benefit as well as mine, finding good opportunities for their horses while trying to ensure, as far as is possible, that I can ride them.

Possibly the most remarkable thing about Dave is his memory - not just for form but for phone numbers. Those who have watched him at work swear that he never needs to pause between calls to look up a number and I can well believe it. I could ring him in late afternoon on his mobile, find him outside taking a well-earned breather and ask him for the number of an obscure permit holder in South Wales, confident that he would rattle off not only his home number but the mobile as well. As one who struggles to memorise half-a-dozen personal numbers, I find it quite amazing. Apparently, they tested Dave out at his local pub once by putting the phone numbers of 100 trainers in envelopes, then getting him to pick 50 at random and identify them. He did not get a single one wrong.

The fact that he is so clearly the best agent in the country might not persuade everyone that it is in so many jockeys' interests to share him. It does sound a weird arrangement yet we actually feed off each other. Martin Pipe, for example, will usually have so many runners at Cheltenham and Aintree that he needs jockeys from outside his yard - Dave can provide them. Similarly, if A.P. is injured or suspended, he often asks Dave to nominate substitutes. The same applies to Nicky Henderson, for whom Mick Fitzgerald is stable jockey, and to Venetia Williams, who uses Norman Williamson. While I was out with a broken leg, the rides on the Hobbs' horses sometimes went to other jockeys in Dave's 'stable', which is not only to the benefit of the agency but also keeps owners happy as they are getting top-class riders.

Just once, in my experience, the sheer scale of the operation caused a fall-out. A few years back, Adrian Maguire left Dave and signed up with a new agent. It was the time when things were going sour for Adrian and it is easy to see why he cast around looking to change things. As, chronologically, he was second only to Guest on the Roberts client-list, and as they had done so much for each other and become correspondingly close friends, Dave was upset at the idea that he might have hurt Adrian or in any way been unfair to him. I don't know whether Adrian regrets leaving but it certainly did him no good. A year later, realising he had made a mistake, he was back on the books and the pair of them are once more great friends.

Dave Roberts takes ten per cent of everything I earn but, as I certainly would earn appreciably less without him, he is worth every penny. My greatest wish is that he should not stop working until I have retired.

Mr. Mulligan

8.

Lessons in disappointment
M r M u l l i g a n

In the summer of 1997, I could have been celebrating my 20th birthday having won both the Cheltenham Gold Cup and Grand National in the same season. History relates that I won neither, and perhaps in terms of keeping my feet on the ground it was just as well, but the fact remains that, not long before their respective defining moments, I had considered both Mr Mulligan and Lord Gyllene to be my rides. The tale of how I came to lose them both is better for the soul than the ego.

Inevitably, I remember him with mixed feelings now, but Mr Mulligan was the first top-class horse I rode and that makes him an important part of my story. It came about through a quite unexpected link-up with his trainer, Noel Chance, a gentle and chatty Irishman with a well-confessed love of a pint of Guinness. I had never heard of him when he first offered me a ride. It was the early summer of 1995 and I was still 17, still an amateur, and spending some time at home with my parents. Noel rang to ask if I was going to Market Rasen on the coming Saturday. The answer was no, but I would be delighted to have the chance. He wanted a 7lb claimer to take some weight off his runner in the valuable handicap hurdle that featured in the course's first summer festival. Monty Royale was the name of the horse and, having his first run for Noel after being bought out of a northern yard, he won by two-and-a-half lengths at 10-1.

Monty Royale's owner, Michael Worcester, employed Noel as his private trainer at the time and, having decided he wanted a jockey on call to ride them all, I was now offered the opening. I don't kid myself that I was first-choice but Mr Worcester did not have sufficient horses to make a claim on a top jockey, so an aspiring claimer was next best. With no commitments to anyone bar the Duke, it was a great break for me and, through it, I began to broaden my knowledge of the Lambourn area in which so many jumpers are trained. I started going down to Noel's yard there once a week to ride out and school and I found him a lovely, relaxed man to work with. I was still wet behind the ears, so Noel did all the talking where Mr Worcester was concerned, and I was very happy that it should stay that way. Over the next couple of seasons, we shared a fair number of winners - but Mr Mulligan was in a class of his own.

I first rode him in September of 1995, three months after my win on Monty Royale. He was an Irish horse and he had won a point-to-point there by a distance before being put into training with Kim Bailey. He had fallen in his only run the previous season, in a hot novice chase at Newbury, and Mr Worcester subsequently switched him to his private operation with Noel, just down the road from Mr Bailey.

Noel is quite fond of running chasing types over hurdles first and he did so with Mr Mulligan. We teamed up in a long-distance novice hurdle at Uttoxeter and he bolted up, making all to win by 15 lengths. Just to rub salt in Kim Bailey's wounds, he trained the favourite, who finished a distant second. I've no idea what potential he had seen in Mr Mulligan but I do know he was not much to look at - he was a common creature in appearance but the striking thing about him was his stride. He covered so much ground, apparently taking one stride to every other horse's two, and although he just stepped over the hurdles he did it very effectively. Noel had told me beforehand that he wasn't very quick but would keep galloping. I came back thinking he was a bit better than advertised. He'd given me a great feel and I raised my eyebrows to Noel as I dismounted, pretty sure we'd got one that would go on and win further races.

Noel likes a bet and I hope and trust he had put the money down at Uttoxeter, because he would not get such a generous price again for some time. Three weeks later, we went to Wetherby with him and frightened off most of the opposition. Only three took him on in a novice hurdle and I was able to make all again, completely unchallenged. Mr Mulligan was now to be switched to the game he was made for, jumping fences, but fate intervened to temporarily separate me from him before his debut.

I turned professional in mid-November, just in time for the big three-day meeting at Cheltenham, but the following weekend I broke my collarbone when coming down at the first in a selling hurdle at Towcester. It was a huge frustration - I had yet to ride my first winner out of amateur status and now I had a spell on the sidelines to endure. Possibly the biggest loss was the ride on Mr Mulligan in the novice chase at Bangor which restarted his fencing career. Mark Dwyer deputised and, starting a short-price favourite, he won by a distance, hacking round and annihilating some pretty weak opposition.

At times like that, having missed a winner on a decent horse, a jockey is always anxious about retrieving the ride, especially when it has been on loan to someone as accomplished as Dwyer. There was the added factor that I was soon to ride out my claim, meaning connections had no weight advantage when they put me up on their horses - a development that has seen the advance of many a young jockey fade and die. Noel and Mr Worcester remained loyal, however, although I now had to wait until mid-January for the horse's next run. He was patently ready to be stepped up in class and the chosen race was a valuable novice chase at Wetherby. The Townton Chase traditionally attracts some high-class chasing recruits and this was no exception. Indeed, the favourite was Call it a Day, sent up by the Duke from Jackdaws Castle having already won once over fences and finished second in a hot contest at Chepstow. The bonus to me from this clash was that I got a lift up to Yorkshire in the helicopter carrying the Duke and Adrian Maguire. On the way, the boss asked me about Mr Mulligan and I told him I rated him pretty highly. The Duke, though, was typically bullish and utterly convinced that Call it a Day would be too good for him.

As it turned out, poor Adrian was injured in the preceding race and Peter Niven took the ride on Call it a Day, but nobody could claim it made the slightest difference to the result. Mr Mulligan won by 15 lengths this time and was so comprehensively superior that I was able to ease him right down on the run-in. Even the Duke now conceded he might not be too bad, though that did not stop him pitching in another of his good novices against him next time out. On this occasion, it was St Mellion Fairway who represented Jackdaws in the grade two Reynoldstown Novices Chase at Ascot in mid-February. Nathen Lad, Major Summit, Go Ballistic and even Lord Gyllene featured among the opposition but they couldn't hold a candle to my horse. Once again, we made all and won unchallenged. once again, 15 lengths was the official margin and I could have made it even bigger if I'd needed to. The *Chaseform* annual for that season reports that Mr Mulligan "treated his rival with contempt in what was certainly the hottest staying novice chase of the season. He is certainly the one they all have to beat in the Sun Alliance Novice Chase."

And that, clearly, was where we would be heading next, which meant I was in a ferment of anticipation for the next month. When Cheltenham finally arrived, Adrian was out injured again and the Duke was good enough to put me on a number of his runners, though nothing with so obviously a chance as Mr Mulligan. He had already beaten most of the best novices seen that season, and beaten them with absolute conviction, so the bookmakers took no chances and shortened him up to 11-8 favourite. An experienced jockey tends to pay very little attention to betting but I was still 18, still awaiting a big breakthrough and naturally impressionable to hype. I think I convinced myself that Mr Mulligan could not get beaten - and that if he did, it must be my fault.

It was the middle day of the Festival, very cold but dry as I remember. The crowd had already roared home two Irish winners and I thought it was time for a British yard (albeit run by a very Irish trainer) to strike a blow. I was right, though not in the way I anticipated. Mr Mulligan, who had jumped so efficiently at Wetherby and Ascot, made a mistake at the first here, which took some wind out of the horse's sails and possibly flustered the jockey. We got back into the race but I still wonder if I was in too much of a hurry to do so. As usual at Cheltenham, the pace was fast and furious and when we made a second mistake midway, it became more of a struggle than I'd been accustomed to on this horse. We got to the front alright but could never shake off Nathen Lad and, whether through the mistakes or the effect of straining for position afterwards, my horse just didn't stride up the final hill as I had dreamt he would. Nathen Lad, a horse we beat pointless at Ascot, came clear by eight lengths and although the rest of the field was in another county to the front two, that was no consolation to me at all. I had been too sure that this race would bring my first Cheltenham winner and now I felt absolutely empty.

The stewards wanted to see me and, just to make the occasion still more painful, they suspended me for four days for 'excessive and improper use of the whip'. Noel and the owner were very good with me, criticising neither the horse nor the way I had ridden him, but I was inconsolable. After racing, I called into the Plough, intending to have a drink with Warren Marston, who had ridden Nathen Lad, but I left quickly, returned to my room at Jackdaws and skulked through the evening, reviewing the race in my mind time and again. I had enjoyed a terrific first season as a professional and was soon to win the conditionals' championship but, in my myopic misery, I felt I had wasted an opportunity that could have taken my career to another level. I really felt I had made a mess of it and, even now, it rates as one of the worst days I have had for disillusionment. I would certainly have felt even worse, had I known that I would never ride Mr Mulligan again.

The following season, I broke my collar-bone again, this time at Chepstow having been unseated when Oatis Rose slipped up on the stable bend. No injury comes at a good time for a jockey but this was especially galling. Ten days later, back on the same course, I had been due to ride Mr Mulligan in the Rehearsal Chase. As it was his first outing since the Cheltenham defeat, I naturally saw it as a chance to put a few things right and silently seethed as the race approached. David Bridgwater was given the ride and they were made favourite but Mr Mulligan ran probably his worst race while in Noel's care, making mistakes and trailing in a well-beaten fourth behind Belmont King. To be honest, he looked a slow horse that day but I knew he could not suddenly have lost all his nerve. If he had to have a bad day, I told myself, it's my good fortune it should come when I was out injured.

His next race was to be the King George VI Chase, Kempton Park's Boxing Day feature, but now a new complication arose for me. David Nicholson had Barton Bank in the King George and Adrian would be there to ride him and the other Kempton runners. But he also wanted to run Call it a Day in the big Christmas race at Wetherby, the Rowland Meyrick Chase, and I was nominated to go there and ride him. I drew a deep breath and told him I had the chance to ride Mr Mulligan at Kempton but he gave a withering response to the effect that he was "nothing but a big, slow boat". I had no option but to ring Noel and tell him the position, knowing that if he could not persuade the Duke to release me, then I would be bound to ride at Wetherby. The Nicholson yard employed me and that was how it worked.

Noel did ring David, but without changing his mind, and I had a nasty feeling what was going to happen next. Sure enough, Noel told me that both he and Mr Worcester wanted a jockey who could commit to riding Mr Mulligan both at Kempton and in the Gold Cup, his ultimate aim. As I was ruled out, they had offered the ride to A.P.McCoy, and as Martin Pipe had no top-class staying chaser likely to produce a clash, he naturally took it with gratitude.

It was a big loss to me and I was inwardly groaning throughout Christmas Day, with no help from excesses of food or drink. I knew I had to buckle down and concentrate on my own rides - and Call it a Day, after all, was a ride most other jockeys would envy - and I set off the following morning with Alan King, the Duke's assistant, at the wheel of the car. It was bitterly cold and we had got as far as the M42 when we heard that the Wetherby meeting had been abandoned for frost. The racing programme, indeed, was being rapidly decimated by the cold snap and, with no chance of picking up rides elsewhere, I was all for heading home. Instead, Alan brightly suggested that we should detour down the M40 and go to watch Barton Bank at Kempton. As this also meant watching Mr Mulligan, it was the last place I wanted to go, as I was gloomily convinced he would win and everyone would put it down to the change of jockey. There was no arguing with Alan, though, so I spent a restless afternoon feeling useless and frustrated until One Man won the King George, somewhat to my relief. I took no pleasure from seeing Mr Mulligan fall, though, and he would certainly have been an honourable second, so I went home that night resigned to the fact that any faint chance I may have had of retrieving the ride had now vanished.

I am not ashamed to say I felt mortified when he won the Gold Cup. I'd just finished second in the first two races on the Cheltenham card, at 40-1 and 25-1, and, not having a ride in the big one, I sat and watched on the weighing-room TV as A.P. drove Mr Mulligan out to win by nine lengths from our own Barton Bank. I could scarcely believe it - not the fact that he had won at 20-1 but that such glory might so easily have been mine. I genuinely wanted to cry and, seeing my confusion, David Bridgwater was the one who came across and consoled me.

I had nobody to blame for what had happened. Racing circumstances caused me to miss out, and A.P. was the beneficiary. Whatever feelings of guilt and inadequacy I had suffered after the Sun Alliance the previous March, I had not been jocked off Mr

Mulligan, but the case of Lord Gyllene was rather different. He was trained at the time by Steve Brookshaw in Staffordshire and his owner was Stan Clarke. I rode for him regularly, both on the horses he had with the Duke (Midnight Legend was the best at that time) and on the Brookshaw horses. Lord Gyllene, a relentless galloper of nine years old who had been bought out in New Zealand, was earmarked for the National at Aintree and, partly in deference to his owner - who runs the course - he was taking the Uttoxeter route there.

He had already won once on his local track, ridden by Tony Dobbin, but when Mr Brookshaw booked me to ride him in the Singer and Friedlander National Trial in early February, I saw it as a chance to pin down a living Aintree chance. Things could hardly have gone any better for us, either, as he won the race by eight lengths, and I fully expected to be on him when he returned to the course for the Midlands National, his final prep race for Aintree. This race is traditionally run on the Saturday following Cheltenham and, having suffered a winless week and the despair of seeing someone else win on Mr Mulligan, it is not difficult to imagine my mood when I found I had been bypassed for the ride on Lord Gyllene and Tony Dobbin was back on board. He was beaten that day but Tony kept the partnership for Aintree and won the Monday National, delayed by two days following the bizarre circumstances of the Saturday bomb scare.

I was never given an explanation for losing that ride, either by the trainer or the owner, and as I was still in the early stages of my career it certainly did not create any publicity. It was something that nagged at me, though, and still does. I felt annoyed, aggrieved, hard done-by - and that was before he won at Aintree. Maybe, if things had been different and I had kept both those rides through to their big days, it would all have gone to my head and I'd have gone the wrong way. I'd have liked the chance, all the same.

Warren Marston

9.

Lasting friendship

Warren Marston

On the day of my first ride under rules, Warren Marston helped play a trick on me that left my confidence in tatters. I sometimes wonder why I ever spoke to him again but the fact is that he has become just about my closest friend in the weighing-room and one of the very few people I will turn to for advice on a racing problem.

The big day for me was to be a Wednesday at Chepstow. Rusty Bridge, the family horse who crops up so often in the early part of my story, was to run in a Hunter Chase and my grandfather was entrusting me with the ride. I had only been working at Jackdaws Castle for about six months and was still wet behind the ears but I told David Nicholson the previous night that I was down for a ride and it was agreed that I would travel to the races with Warren, who had been around a few years as a jockey and was then riding pretty prolifically as a freelance.

Next morning, I was down to ride two lots, as usual, but after first lot Warren said we had to get moving. Diffidently - I was only 16 and extremely shy - I went to the head lad, Clifford Baker, to check I could go. It felt like being back at school, asking the teacher for permission to go home early, and Clifford managed to make me feel very small. When we finally got on the road, Warren said we had a stop to make on the way as he was due to school some horses for Chris Broad, then a trainer at Westbury-on-Severn but subsequently to become a jockeys' agent.

At the time, I had barely heard of Chris, let alone met him, and his singular sense of humour was a mystery to me. Warren, though, used to ride all his horses and was that afternoon due to partner the very useful Mudahim (who later won a *Racing Post* Chase) in his first novice chase. After a chat between the two of them, in which Warren gave me what I took to be a flattering build-up, Chris said I should make myself useful by joining in the schooling session.

He indicated the horse I was to ride and said I should lead Warren down over a set of mini-hurdles. Naively, I got on board and attempted to follow instructions, only for my mount to pull up mulishly and refuse to cross a flight. With a bit of grumbling from the watching trainer and a spot of embarrassment from yours truly, I set off again and the same thing happened. Chris now impatiently directed us towards a set of logs on the floor but this recalcitrant creature would not even jump one of those.

My confidence had now hit the deck with a mighty thud. I had thought I might even be in the market for a spare ride from Chris if I made a decent impression but instead, patently, I had made a fool of myself. Nothing much was said and the journey to Chepstow continued with the passenger in contemplative mood. It was only the following day, after a spot of chuckling back at Jackdaws between Warren and Gordon Clarkson, that I found out I had been set up. The horse I was riding was a mulish flat handicapper who had never left the ground. It had been their idea of a joke at my expense.

All of which might give a mistaken impression of Warren. If it was in his mind that day to keep my feet firmly on the ground, he has ever since been there for me in a very constructive way. He put in words for me with various trainers (apart from the mischievous Broad) when I was trying to get started and if ever I had a problem I found it easy to go and speak to him, either around the yard or when we were out socially. Even if it was something trifling, he would never put me down. In what is such a highly competitive, ever cutthroat business, this is a very rare quality.

He still calls me 'Young', the name he gave me when I first turned up at the Duke's emporium, but nowadays I notice him taking time to encourage jockeys far younger and more impressionable than I have become. If a new lad comes into the weighing-room, full of shy anxiety, Warren will invariably be the first to go across for a chat to put him at his ease. Not everyone can carry that off - I find it difficult making a conversation out of nothing with someone I don't know - but it comes naturally to the confident personality of W.Marston and it must mean a great deal to any newcomer to have someone as widely recognised and respected as he is taking time out to say hello.

Warren worked full-time for the Duke during my first year, living in with the rest of us, and even after he moved to a house in Little Rissington he was still in the yard three mornings a week and we would see plenty of him in the stable local, The Plough, each weekend. I had quickly started getting pretty regular rides and he was forever offering me a lift to the races, which was a big help for someone who did not find it easy asking around for favours.

One day, going racing, I remember him saying to me that you must always keep the small trainers happy, because you never know when you will need them. He is living proof of this himself, because after three years of riding for Jenny Pitman's high-profile yard in Lambourn he lost his job and has since been confined to picking up whatever he can as a hard-working freelance. His career never quite took off as it might have done but he has been anything but a failure. One March, he rode two Cheltenham Festival winners - Nathen Lad and Indefence - for Mrs Pitman and I really thought that would prove his launch pad. Instead, he spent the following season frustrated, telling us that she had so many lovely horses that just weren't firing.

If he had gone on to ride a Gold Cup winner, or even a National winner for the Pitman yard it might have worked out very differently. He did ride plenty of winners in his time there but her horses were probably seldom at their best at that stage. Warren is also someone who likes to put his opinion across and I can imagine that it did not always tally with that of Mrs P. When a yard begins to struggle, it is invariably the jockey who takes the majority of blame. Warren, I know, found things very hard during his last year with Jenny, because he was constantly on good horses that did not produce their true form. Few things are more frustrating for a jockey than that. Having lost such a good job, though, a lot of jockeys would have gone into rapid freefall and been retired within two or three years. Warren, who still loved the life, has refused to let that happen to him.

Through sheer endeavour, he has built a portfolio of rides from trainers around the country. Most of them are small yards but he has also begun riding a good deal for the Yorkshire stable of Sue Smith and I can just imagine him putting the world to rights with Sue's ever-opinionated husband, Harvey. Warren is clocking up as many winners as he ever did and it is all a testimony to his willingness to work - partly in getting on the road at ungodly hours to ride out for all these people but also the energy he puts into every ride. If there are those who say similar things about my riding, then much of the credit resides with Warren, for this is one of the things he instilled in me very early.

Something he does better than me, I think, is assessing the form and pace of every race and riding his horse accordingly. He is a fine tactical rider. Often, you might see him finish third or fourth on a rank outsider because he has given it an intelligent ride rather than simply accepting he could not win and going through the motions. Owners and trainers - especially those who do not have winners every week - like that sort of thing, which accounts for his continuing popularity.

He is a very good man to school with (I am generously discounting the Chris Broad episode here) and one of the best in the weighing-room at assessing the strengths of a race. Even now, if I am fretting about the ride I gave a horse, or wondering about the quality of a race I have won, I will go to one of two people for an opinion - Warren or the Duke. I trust the judgement of them both. Sometimes, Warren will warn me not to get carried away with the form of a horse because the race will not stand the test of time. Usually, he is right.

Warren is not beyond losing his temper on the racecourse. He gets frustrated, I think, and if he gets cut up in a race his voice will be heard clearly and loudly. He's certainly not the fighting type, though, and if he had not become a jockey I think he would like to have been a singer. I imagine he was in the choir at Millfield School, where he was also a proficient all-round sportsman, and he has frequently enjoyed advertising his voice at the bar of the Plough, rounding off a sociable Saturday night with a rousing rendition of Meat Loaf's 'Bat Out of Hell'.

Socially great fun, he is domestically a shambles. His mother runs a bed-and-breakfast place at Broadway and Warren, apparently unable to look after himself, has moved back in there. He is so useless in practical terms that I sometimes suspect his Mum runs his life and give him weekly spending money. If his car goes wrong, or he needs to re-programme his mobile phone, he is utterly clueless and the peak of his culinary powers was tested recently when he bought a ready-made lasagne for his supper. He appeared smugly in the Plough that night, informing us that the packet has said he should put it in a hot oven so he had switched on and left it to warm up. Two hours later, his electric oven having been shedding power and money needlessly, he left the pub to cook his great supper. Nobody volunteered to share it with him and I think it would need a very brave woman to move in and share his inefficiency. So far as the lads in the weighing-room are concerned, though, he can stay around as long as he likes - not that we would ever tell him so.

Anzum

10.

When push comes to shove

A   n   z   u   m

The majority of horses will be fleeting companions for a jockey, some remembered fondly, others not. Anzum, though, was a long term affair, not always easy to be with, often very hard work but ultimately one of the most fulfilling relationships of my career. He was eight years old when he gave me my first winner at the Cheltenham Festival, in the most dramatic fashion imaginable. By then, though, he had been part of my life for almost six years. Looking back to how it all began, I could never have dreamed the ending.

The partnership was forged in 1993, not long after I started out with David Nicholson, but it started to become special in the autumn of 1994. I was into my second year at Jackdaws by then and, after the usual probationary period in which I had been trusted with nothing beyond the basics, I was allowed to start demonstrating if I had any aptitude for schooling. Anzum was my first partner. He belonged to Colin Smith, along with another horse called Secret Hobby, and although both had run on the flat as two-year-olds, neither had won and Secret Hobby looked to be virtually devoid of ability.

They had been ridden out by Xavier Aizpura and myself for the best part of a year and I definitely had the better half of the deal. Secret Hobby was a horrible horse, who took the mickey out of his riders, ducking and diving on gallops with an evil pleasure. He buried 'Shav' more than once and when it came to the time to start schooling the pair of them for juvenile hurdles, I think 'Shav' was not quite as delighted as me when the Duke told us we could keep the rides.

It was to be a mutual education process - us teaching them to jump while they, unwittingly, taught us the rudiments of how to school. It was an early sign of being given some responsibility in the yard but, in truth, it was probably also a sign that there were no lofty expectations for either horse. Anzum, having at least finished second on the flat, was doubtless marked down as one who should be capable of winning a little race if he took to hurdles, but what followed over the years shows how infrequently flat form can be equated to the jumps.

The schooling process was simple and repetitive. There were lines of logs and mini-hurdles set up on the all-weather gallop at Jackdaws and we went up and down there twice a week, every week. Secret Hobby was the first to go to the racecourse and was duly tailed off in a poor event, confirming the common opinion of him, but Anzum was seen as more of a long term project and I schooled him religiously for two months before the Duke decided he was ready to run. He started with the sights low, sending him to Bangor-on-Dee, where even in a modest three-year-old race he did not go off favourite. He won by nine lengths, though, and I remember Warren coming back full of praise for his jumping, which gave me the kick of feeling I had contributed something to the result.

Next time out, he beat a hotshot of Martin Pipe's at Newbury and he was now clearly going places. He was heading, in fact, to become one of the equine celebrities of that winter, because under the piloting of Warren (three times), Adrian (twice) and Rob Massie, he won six consecutive juvenile hurdles and was promoted favourite for the generation's championship race, the Triumph Hurdle at Cheltenham. His two most striking runs were probably the last in the sequence of six, at Nottingham and Newbury, where he dominated from flagfall on the deep ground he evidently adored. He was lucky in that Cheltenham was soft too, something of a rarity in modern times, but in a field of 26, with so many wanting to make the pace, he could never get near the front. Warren rode him, (Adrian was in Ireland after the shock death of his mother, the first of many Cheltenhams he was to miss) and, in a preview of what awaited me in later seasons, he had to shove him along through the race to stay in touch. He finished flying in fourth and was subsequently placed third after the disqualification of the runner-up. Just over an hour later, following the Gold Cup win of Master Oats, I had my second festival ride of the week on Sandybraes in the Foxhunters. He pulled up, yet Anzum's efforts still sent me home thinking it was a good day, and wondering if I would ever get the chance to ride him myself.

It was a longish wait, but worth every minute. The following season, the Duke upped him in trip, first to two-and-a-half miles at Chepstow, where he made no show, and then a further two furlongs at Sandown, where he finished third on unsuitably quick ground. Whether or not that was responsible, he came back with a leg problem and did not run for virtually a year. When he won on his comeback, late in 1996, Warren was on him again but I had my first ride on Anzum early in February the following year. It was

Chepstow and the ground was soft but the one factor against him was the two-and-a-half mile trip. It was now short of his optimum and he showed it, rallying on the run-in to finish a close third behind Brave Tornado.

It may seem incongruous that a horse quick enough to win six juvenile hurdles was now crying out for a marathon trip but it is actually not so unusual. As a rule, the three and four-year old hurdles are run at a punishing gallop which brings stamina into play. Just as those who do well often need to go up in trip soon afterwards, horses who do not win as juveniles can come into their own in ordinary novice hurdles the following year, partly through late maturing but also because such races are frequently run at a more sedate pace.

Anzum was now earmarked for the Stayers Hurdle at Cheltenham but I did not expect to ride him. My chance at Chepstow had come because Adrian was on a host of stable fancies at Warwick. He was the retained jockey and he had, as usual, a great deal to anticipate at the Festival - except that Adrian, having missed it for two previous years, may already have given up looking forward too far. Cruelly it was to happen again, as a fall from a debutant novice chaser at Leicester at the end of February broke his arm. His immense popularity ensured that the first emotion of everyone at Jackdaws was sympathy for such wretched misfortune. But the racing business waits for no-one and, for the third year running, the Duke had to make alternative riding plans for the biggest week of the season. This year for the first time, I was to be one of the prime beneficiaries.

I had my first ride on the Triumph Hurdle on a 100-1 shot, Zabadi, and 'Chocolate' Thornton rode a double for the Duke later on the Tuesday card. Wednesday brought me closer to that first

Festival win - I was fourth behind Istabraq in the Sun Alliance Hurdle, then rode two thirds before finishing runner-up in the bumper to a promising Irish five-year-old called Florida Pearl. As a 19-year-old, I suppose I should have been overjoyed by so many great rides at Cheltenham but I longed for a winner and my frustration increased when I was beaten a length in the Triumph Hurdle, the opening race of Thursday's programme. As Circus Star, my mount, went off at 40-1, and the winner was Commanche Court, this was another exceptional run and in 24 hours I had now chased up three horses who were to become legends in the ensuing years - Istabraq, Florida Pearl and Commanche Court.

The Stayers came next and Anzum, too, was a long-shot, partly because the Duke had a much better fancied contender in Estartefique, ridden by David Bridgwater, but also because the ground was fast. Predictably, Anzum got taken off his feet in the middle of the race and, had he been any other horse, you would have said he was tailing off. I knew 'Bridgie' had committed too far out on Escartefique though, and although he was still in front going to the last, the cavalry was closing. Karshi took it up and went away up the hill to win for Lord Vesty, the Cheltenham Chairman, but Anzum, having flown down the hill, raced back up it like a lion and would have won in another 100 yards.

Compared to all that excitement, I had a pretty quiet Cheltenham the following year, when Adrian finally got to ride at the meeting. There was no winners for me, and no Anzum - he had suffered further leg problems and was given the year off. When that happens to a good horse, there is always the fear that he won't come back or, if he does, that he will be nowhere near the force of old. The residual damage may be physical but might equally be mental, with a horse having suffered some pain on the course and then losing his routine for a long period and finding it hard to summon enthusiasm for doing it all over again. Anzum was one of the fortunate ones - or, perhaps more accurately, we were fortunate with him.

Not that his early comeback runs filled us with confidence. As a young horse, he had been easy to get fit and ran well fresh but it was different now. Possibly the Duke had deliberately taken it easy with him after the injury, but in his first two races he was beaten an aggregate of 130 lengths and widely written off as a light of his former days. Most people were not inclined to soften that view when he went to Kempton and finished third behind his stablemate Pharanear, but I felt that was a good run on a course that did not suit him. There were signs, to me, that he was coming back to his best and, as I was definitely booked to ride him at the Festival, I allowed myself to believe he had an each-way chance.

The same opinion was voiced - though, in his own way, more loudly - by the Duke when he went to Ireland for a pre-Cheltenham panel. The audience and fellow panel members were scornful, saying it was a weak Stayers in which he would finish second and that this year's renewal was in a different class. Well, on paper they were right - certainly, with Deano's Beeno and Lady Rebecca representing top British form and Le Coudray reckoned to be an Irish banker, it was a highly competitive betting race. Anzum was out with the washing at 40-1 but the Duke, riled by the mockery, struck a very public £50 each-way with the Irish bookmaker Sean Graham. In the days that followed, one of our local Cotswold bookies, a man who used to come into The Plough regularly, also took a disproportionate number of bets on Anzum as the yard's confidence grew.

Anzum was not a good mover by this stage and I had no great hopes of being able to keep him up with the pace. Predictably, A.P.

McCoy set off in front on Deeno's Beeno, with Lady Rebecca tracking and Charlie Swan holding up Le Coudray. I was not far from him but I was not deliberately holding up Anzum but asking him to go as fast as he could. He is the sort of horse a jockey could never entirely give up on, such was his stamina and courage, but with a circuit to go I could see no possible way we could win. It was a long way around, the second time, as Anzum saw no point in working unless his jockey put in a considerable amount of effort. He didn't want hitting, and certainly went no faster for it, but you had to keep pushing, cajoling and encouraging. Going to the top of the hill, a mile from home, I was still 25 lengths off the leaders but the optimist in me was insisting that this race was not over - I still thought I had a chance of being placed and, as if sensing the same thing, Anzum was picking up the bridle.

It had suited me that the three principals, wary of each other, had turned the race into the sort of slog that brought Anzum's greatest virtues into play. Deano's had no more to give after the second last and it must then have looked from the stands as if it was settling into a duel between Lady Rebecca and Le Coudray - Britain against Ireland, the mare against the gelding. Venetia Williams and some hugely enthusiastic Herefordshire owners against Aidan O'Brien and J.P. McManus. The neutrals were probably rooting for the local underdog but the Irish would have shouted them down. Whatever, very few will have noticed the striped silks of Anzum making suddenly rapid progress through the also-rans.

At the last, I was confident I'd be third but there was still ten lengths to find with the leaders - a mountain on that run-in. He was digging deep, though, and while I realise it was a relative experience - the slowing of the horses in front contributed to the sensation - I suddenly felt we were going much quicker than I'd thought Anzum was capable of. Halfway up the hill, still pushing for all I was worth, we went past the weakening Lady Rebecca. The next time I dared to take a peek, Le Coudray seemed to be stopping in front of me. I'm sure Charlie must have thought he had won after seeing off the mare and it must have surprised him to hear me arriving from nowhere. By then though, there was nothing he could do. His horse was a spent force and we sailed past in the shadow of the post.

What do you feel like when you've finally ridden your first Cheltenham winner? Exhausted, in my case. I remember standing up in my irons and twisting my face into something between a grin of joy and a grimace of pain. I knew it had been special but it was only much later, watching it on video, that the drama of the victory really registered. We had come from such a long way back, that the Duke, watching from his usual position on the lawn, had seen us jump the last then headed for the winners' enclosure, sure we would be no better than third. As he neared the paddock someone said 'well done' to him but he still needed convincing that he should be diverting to the number one slot.

The party that night was pretty memorable too, or so I am told. The local paper sent a photographer along at 8.30pm, while I was still in a reasonable state, but some subversive alternative pictures were taken of me much later and pinned up in the pub for the next few weeks, a reminder of how rough I looked. I had prudently arranged to have the next morning free from riding out but there was still the matter of a single booked ride at Folkestone. Folkestone, of all places. I lay in bed, head pounding, throat dry and mentally raging about the idiocy of staging meetings at Folkestone and Fakenham the day after Cheltenham. I was still trying to summon the strength to stir when the bedside phone rang. It was

Dave Roberts, telling me my horse was a non-runner. I never expected to feel so relieved at hearing such news, though I wondered fleetingly if the owners had taken the precaution after visualising my post-race party.

I received the Ride of The Year award for the Stayers but I was equally pleased with a very different ride I gave him the following month, at Punchestown. Knowing that Irish races are habitually run at a slower pace, I suggested to the Duke that we made all the running, just as he had done with such success as a juvenile. I knew he would enjoy it in front so long as he could get his own way and, with Deano's Beeno not in the field and Le Coudray a regular hold-up horse, I was pretty confident they'd leave me alone. I got him motivated at the start, as I knew I would need to in this reversion of tactics, but he set off with a spring in his stride that confirmed his confidence was high, having won a race for the first time in more than two years. A lot of people on the course, I'm told, were convinced that I had gone off too fast through the first two miles and were certain that I would come back to the field, but as he turned into the straight he put his head down and went again. Le Coudray had been pulled-up and the challenge came from another J.P. McManus horse, Khayrawani, who had won handicaps at both Cheltenham and Aintree. Anzum, though, was not to be denied.

The Duke's retirement came later that year and, although Anzum kept running for Alan King and subsequently Richard Phillips, he did not contest another Stayers Hurdle - niggling injuries saw to that. He did, though, turn in one further herculean performance, in the Long Walk Hurdle at Ascot in December of 1999. Deano's Beeno was thought to be a certainty that day - he was sent off the 4-9 favourite - and it was a war of attrition throughout the three mile-plus trip. The favourite led most of the way but Anzum never let him out of his sights. Two out, we took up the running and my horse forged clear to win by almost twenty lengths. That day he advertised all his best assets of toughness and courage. It was to be the last race he won, and it is a good way to remember him.

Adrian Maguire

11.

Riding the rollercoaster

A d r i a n   M a g u i r e

It was the Saturday before Cheltenham and I was feeling sorry for myself, the untimely irritation of a head cold compounded by three consecutive fancied rides making no show at Chepstow. Plodding back to the weighing-room, sniffling and coughing, after the third - my potential National mount Billingsgate - had pulled up with a broken blood vessel, it was one of those disaffected moments when I fleetingly felt like giving up. It never lasts, of course, and by the end of the afternoon I was feeling ashamed of the notion for two reasons. My own working day had ended with a couple of winners, after all. Adrian Maguire's day had ended in hospital, the very last place any jockey wants to visit on the most expectant weekend of the season.

At first, none of us knew how bad it would turn out for him. There is an efficient grapvine system among the jockeys and I was told of Adrian's predicament when I met up with a few other lads in The Plough early that evening. He had been riding an old three-mile chaser called Luzcadou at Warwick and initially it was thought that the fall might have broken his arm. That, in itself, would have been a barely believable reprise of the injury that started his Cheltenham hoodoo back in 1995 - the first of three consecutive festivals he was to miss. But it was worse than that, much worse. By Sunday morning, when the Cotswold jockeys gathered for lunch, we knew that Adrian had broken a bone in his neck. The only good news was that he had escaped paralysis. The bad news was that he would not ride for many months.

To say it cast a pall over the lunch table hardly does it justice. It was horrible news - next to a death in the family, almost the worst imaginable. They said the pain from the injury was under control but I bet they could not say the same about the pain from his immediate loss. Missing Cheltenham yet again, and in a year when he had been back riding with all his old poise and purpose, was a grotesque stroke of fate, made all the worse because Adrian is just such a nice fellow. It would be ludicrous to say any of us would have volunteered to change places with him but if such a hideous injury, so callously timed, had to happen to somebody, I think we would all have have wished it on anybody but Adrian. It just seemed so dreadfully unfair.

Thinking back, that weekend was full of fate and coincidence. On the Friday night, Zara and I had gone to London for a benefit dinner for Richard Dunwoody. One of the greatest of jump jockeys, Richard's career was shortened by a neck injury he could not cure, and by the weakening effect it had on an arm. Retirement does not come easy in this game and I know many ex-jockeys who have struggled to come to terms with it, though none who have taken it to the lengths that Richard has done, cutting himself off from racing almost entirely. At that dinner, the auction demonstrated his determination for a new life as he publicly sold off his old riding equipment. I found it all rather sad. Dunwoody always had his own way of doing things, on and off horseback, and few people probably felt very close to him. He was a fantastic jockey, much the best of his time, and I just wish he could enjoy it more. When the 2002 Cheltenham festival began, Richard was yet again conspicuous by his absence - he just won't come and watch. Striking a stark contrast, Adrian Maguire, whose finest season still ended in a shadow cast by Dunwoody, lay in a Coventry hospital awaiting a second operation on his neck.

Adrian's first year as stable jockey to David Nicholson, 1992-93, was the season I joined the yard at the bottom. I knew he'd won the Gold Cup the previous year but as my newspaper reading as a child was confined to headlines and pictures, I knew nothing else about him. The next season, however, he carried all before him - or nearly did. In early spring he looked certain to be champion jockey and, after another two Cheltenham winners, he jumped the last fence in the Grand National in front on Moorcroft Boy. That, in a sense, was as good as it got. Moorcroft Boy, who had burst a blood vessel during the race, was caught on that unforgiving run-in, beaten by a horse called Minnehoma and a jockey called Dunwoody. Over the next two months, Dunwoody pursued Maguire relentlessly for the championship and, just as in the National, got up to win on the final run to the line. It was a gripping battle which the public followed with a sustained devotion seldom given to jump racing, but it must have taken a lot out of both men and the worst of it was that the loser never did get another fair crack. Injuries made certain of that - all bad enough, usually breaks and almost invariably at the most inopportune times. For Adrian, it was to be a very long wait for another Cheltenham Festival and when he did get out there in 1998 it ended in yet more pain and disillusionment when he was buried at the fence in front of the stands during the Grand Annual Chase. I remember the concern of everyone (he even knows what the thousands watching from the stands were thinking) as he lay motionless and those dreaded green screens were erected around him. He got away, if that is an appropriate phrase, with just a bad dose of concussion and a broken collar-bone and even then, his humour shone through. Recalling the sights of the screens going up, some time later, he chuckled and said: "People thought they were going to shoot me."

Adrian has needed a lot of humour to get through his misfortunes with injury, and a great deal of patience. He had to summon the same virtues both during and after his split with David Nicholson, a situation that affected me directly and left me worrying - needlessly, thanks to Adrian - about our relationship. I had learned very early on about Adrian's patience, though, and how he applied it so effectively to his riding.

He was, quite simply, the best schooling jockey I had ever seen and I've no reason to doubt that he still is. Little was said between us when we first met at Jackdaws Castle, because I was shy and Adrian just instinctively quiet, but when we were out with the string in the mornings I would watch him closely and try to take in the lessons. The Duke's way was to school all the novices at the start of each season and all the bumper horses at the end. An area of the schooling grounds was set out for this primary education, with logs and small hurdles set out. Day after day, Adrian would get on these ignorant animals, big and backward National Hunt thoroughbreds, yet within ten minutes he would have them responding like showjumpers.

Frankly, I was in awe of this skill but I came to realise it flowed his relaxed manner on a horse. Although very small himself, he always looked part of the horse rather than just a passenger, flowing with their movements and never panicking them by rushing or yanking their heads around. If one was coming into the obstacles crooked, he wouldn't pull it about but just quietly trot a circle before coming in again. The horses quickly picked up confidence from him and I am sure it would be a very good education for all young jockeys to watch him. Certainly, I have picked up many tips from Adrian over the years and I think my riding has improved for it. I never saw Dunwoody or John Francome school and I'm sure they must have been very good but I've never come across anyone as impressive as Adrian.

It was fully two seasons before I felt I knew him properly but this was not through any standoffishness on his part. In my first year, I didn't school at all (though occasionally I would get to watch) and it was well into my second before we spent enough time together for me to pick up the verbal tips from him as well as those I got just from observing his riding. On occasions, we would travel to racing in the same car and he was always helpful, though once I had been around him a while I knew better than to expect a constant flow of conversation - he just isn't like that.

Adrian and 'The Duke' had been a good partnership for some years. In hindsight, I am sure David would readily acknowledge that. For their first three seasons together they seemed to get along famously and it was a mutually rewarding match-up. David's horses were in good form and Adrian kept giving them terrific rides. He got such tunes out of horses that he could be two or three lengths down at the last and still conjure up a winning run from an apparently beaten horse. Nowadays, A.P.McCoy gets every record, every accolade but when Adrian was in his purple patch it was hard to believe anyone could ride better.

I really have no idea why they fell out, or, at least, what the original source of the problem was. Of course, Adrian had suffered a lot of time out through injury - if I'd been laid up so often, I honestly think I would have retired - and I know from experience how hard it is to come back to race-riding and carry on just as it was before. Having said that, I did not discern Adrian riding any differently after those injuries and if his performance did dip at all it was more likely to be through a lack of confidence born of the uncertainty all around him.

Much as I like and respect David Nicholson, I do not think this was one of his finest episodes. I was not privileged to what went on between them or who said what and when, but it did seem to be a situation that should have been handled better. Everybody falls out with somebody, that is a fact of life, but if both of them were honest about it now I wonder if it all began with something very petty that they could easily have sorted out with better communication.

Whatever the true facts, one part of the developing situation that escaped nobody was the benefits that were coming my way. As the Duke showed his dissatisfaction by replacing Adrian on an ever-increasing number of his horses, most of the rides were coming to me. It helped my career a lot, so perversely I have to be grateful. At the time, though, my dominant emotions were embarrassment at how it was happening, and anxiety that Adrian would take out his grievances on me.

In his position, I know I would have found it difficult, seeing someone else in the yard - someone younger and less accomplished - taking my rides. I'm not sure how I might have reacted but I doubt I could have mustered the dignity Adrian showed. Around the yard, he never gave any hint as to what was going on and, with me, he was fantastic - not so much as a single cross or frustrated word. Occasionally, I felt I had to ask him about a ride I had 'inherited' from him and I feared a rebuff, yet he was always helpful, telling me things about the horses that only he could have known. My respect for him, already high, soared during those weeks and months.

Leaving Jackdaws was eventually his only option and there were those who thought his career would shrivel afterwards. Instead, through linking up with his long-time friend Ferdy Murphy, whose Yorkshire yard is now one of the biggest in the north, he has restored his self-belief and brought the quality of his riding back to general attention. He is a very hard man to ride against and if I find myself in a battle with him from the last I can sense that coiled drive alongside me getting every ounce of effort from his horse. As one of the most liked people in the weighing-room, his recent successes have been widely popular and, even though I was laid up with a broken leg, it was great to see him win the King George VI Chase at Kempton last Christmas through such a positive ride on Florida Pearl. I had ridden the horse before, might have been offered the ride had I been fit, but if I could have nominated anyone else to win on him, it would certainly have been Adrian.

His broken neck was scary, the sort of injury that jockeys just don't like contemplating, yet to see him the following month was amazing. He came to Aintree, then to the finale meeting at Sandown, and although his upper body was encased in a metal brace, with pins drilled through his head to keep the bones in place, he has still managed to laugh and joke with us. It would have been all too easy for him to be self-absorbed, depressed about his fate, even defeatist about a career that has suffered so many setbacks. Instead, he evidently could not wait to get back riding.

If ever I am down, about a lack of winners or a heavy fall or simple fatigue, I can think of Adrian and put things in perspective. Anyone who can come through all his misfortune and still show the spirit and fortitude that he does is inspiring to the entire profession.

Looks Like Trouble

12.
Triumph by Chance
Looks Like Trouble

Three years after losing the ride on Mr Mulligan, I finally won the Gold Cup for Noel Chance - and this time, the roles were spookily reversed. There was no question of Looks Like Trouble being my ride, or indeed anyone's ride bar Norman Williamson, until a matter of days before Cheltenham. To this day, I am not fully aware of the reasons why Norman was removed from the horse and, natural sympathy apart, it is not my business. Norman's misfortune brought me the greatest windfall of my career and, though it may seem greedy to say so, I feel slightly aggrieved it resulted in only one Gold Cup rather than the two or three that the horse perhaps deserved.

Michael Worcester began cutting back on his horses in 1997. Perhaps winning the Gold Cup had sated his ambition, I just don't know. He had no further need of a private trainer, anyway, which not only left Noel to seek new premises of his own but left me with one fewer string to my riding bow. I have always found Noel an honest and honourable man and he told me straight that I might as well stop my weekly trips to Lambourn to school for him as there would be little left for me to ride. In the next couple of years, I probably had an average of one ride every six months for him and, while I missed his engaging company, things were going well enough for me elsewhere not to be missing his winners.

Looks Like Trouble, though, was a horse that everyone in the weighing-room would have begged to ride and it reflected enormous credit on Noel, who has never been among the biggest trainers in terms of numbers yet was producing a Gold Cup winner for the second time in four years. I know now, from renewed contact with him, that he had always maintained immense faith in Looks Like Trouble and had been scornful of the many who underrated him, labelling his previous Cheltenham win in the 1999 Sun Alliance Chase as a fluke and belabouring his earlier jumping frailties as a reason for dismissing him in the highest grade. After proving such cynics wrong once again, Noel is entitled to think that only the foolish will mock next time he says he has a Gold Cup horse.

Not that it had always been obvious that Looks Like Trouble was destined for great things. He was bought, like many of Noel's horses, out of the Irish point-to-pointing scene, in which he has many sound contacts, but the one thing that could be said after his first season in England was that he was not going to make a hurdler. He was beaten in novice events at Carlisle, Folkestone and Exeter, ridden on each occasion by Seamus Durack, who had inherited the majority of the rides in the Chance stable.

Put over fences relatively early in life, aged six, Looks Like Trouble fell in his first chase and was beaten out of sight in his next two, albeit behind very useful opposition. The rest of the story, though, is the stuff of racing dreams. He won his three remaining starts in that 1998-99 season, culminating with the Sun Alliance, in which he belied odds of 16-1. That race, though, was reported and remembered for all the wrong reasons - the injury suffered by the Irish-trained favourite, Nick Dundee, after a crashing fall at the third-last fence had put a premature end to a developing duel between the pair. It was because of that, and the ensuing drama over whether Nick Dundee could be saved to race again, that Looks Like Trouble never received the credit he was due for winning a championship race run at such a punishing pace that only the two of them were left in contention when the favourite fell.

Noel may have resented the faint praise but he turned it to his advantage, preparing his horse in relative peace for the following year's Gold Cup and, doubtless, availing himself of some over-generous odds along the way. Meantime, Norman Williamson, who had ironically been committed to Nick Dundee in the Sun Alliance, was engaged to ride the horse, who started out with a respectable third in the Charlie Hall Chase and followed up with a facile win at Sandown before running no sort of race in the King George VI Chase, where Norman pulled him up at halfway.

I rode Go Ballistic that day and he finished a remote second to the impressive See More Business, but while we were all surprised by the impotence of Looks Like Trouble - who went off as second favourite - jockeys know better than anyone that horses do not necessarily perform to order. He had a bad day, for whatever reason, and that seemed an end to it. Subsequent speculation seems to centre on this race as the source of the fall-out between Norman and the owner, Tim Collins, but if that is the case it seems strange that Norman was still on board at Cheltenham at the end of January, when Looks Like Trouble slaughtered five opponents in the Pillar Chase. Again, I was on Go Ballistic, ever the bridesmaid and consigned to second place once more - this time, however, I was barely in the same county as Norman's horse and everyone now marked him down as the best British-based alternative to See More Business for the Gold Cup.

During the week before Cheltenham, I was serving a suspension, so took up an invitation to go to Ireland for a few days, mixing in a pre-Festival panel with a spot of golf and relaxation at the excellent Dunraven Arms Hotel in Adare. The panel was staged on the Sunday evening and, as ever in those parts, it was a lively occasion. David Nicholson is something of a local hero over there and, despite having handed over the training licence to Alan King, he was ritually talking up the prospects of the Jackdaws Castle runners. I happily went along with this angle, as I was down to ride most of them, and we both gave a favourable mention to the each-way chance of Splendid in the Gold Cup.

Splendid had finished second to Ever Blessed in the Hennessy Gold Cup that season, and run respectably at Ascot afterwards, but in my heart I had serious doubts whether he was up to Gold Cup standard. I had no alternative ride in the race, though, and so I cheerfully sung his praises, simultaneously talking down the prospects of Looks Like Trouble on the basis of his poor run at Kempton. The things we say...

The following morning, I was about to go and play a round of golf with Luke Harvey, the ex-jockey turned racing television presenter, when Dave Roberts rang me on the mobile. He told me to expect a call from Noel Chance offering me the ride on Looks Like Trouble. I knew it wasn't a wind-up (Dave doesn't joke about things like that) but even when I had read, a couple of days earlier, that Norman was going to lose the ride it had not registered with me that I would now be in line. Hastily discarding the opinions I had expressed the previous evening, I took the call from Noel, told him I would be thrilled to ride and then set about obtaining my release from Splendid. In the event, he was diverted to the William Hill Handicap Chase on the opening day and, as he could only finish fifth behind Marlborough, it was clearly correct, as well as convenient for me, to have missed the Gold Cup with him.

Once I got home from Ireland I went down to Lambourn and schooled Looks Like Trouble over three fences. After that, the marvellous madness of the best three days of the year was upon me and there was really no time to sit back and analyse the ride I had acquired. Sometimes, this can be a good thing for a jockey. If you do not know a horse well, or feel deeply involved in its preparation, you basically turn up and do as the trainer tells you, your mind clear of all peripheral concerns. Having weeks and months to build up to a fancied ride in a big race is not always beneficial to the mental state.

I was aware that I had done nothing to deserve such a chance, apart perhaps from my earlier in involvement with Noel's stable, and there was an inevitable sense of discomfort about Norman's position. Having suffered something similar, to my way of thinking, with Lord Gyllene in the 1997 National, I felt I had some idea how he was feeling but it remains a difficult thing to approach someone when you are on their horse. Whatever had gone on was plainly not my fault, yet I could not help but feel a little bit guilty. When it was over, and the horse had won, Norman could not have behaved better. He came to congratulate me and made it clear that this was something between him and the owner, quite definitely nothing for me to worry about. He didn't tell me the full story and I'm not entirely sure he knows it himself, but both parties have kept the matter private and, in such difficult circumstances, that is how it should be. I suspect I will go through something similar in years to come - in a game that comes down to personal opinion, it is waiting to happen for us all.

Though he won the Gold Cup by five lengths, it did not entirely go according to plan. Knowing that the pace would be strong, Noel had told me not to try and rush him to the front but settle him in behind the leaders and make my challenge between the last two fences. Heading down the back straight for the last time, though, I felt he had gone to sleep. He made one bad mistake and I had to draw the stick on him a couple of times just to get his mind back on the job. He was a very big horse and tended, at the time, to go round some of his races in a dream - maybe that is what happened at Kempton that Christmas. Certainly, there was a stage of the race when I was not happy but when he did respond it was decisive. We will never know what might have happened if Gloria Victis had not fallen fatally two, having made all the running. Tony McCoy, who was distraught for some time afterwards, is adamant he might still have won but my impression is that he was beaten. Florida Pearl was left in front but I took his measure at the last and, going up the hill, there was only one possible winner.

There are days when a big winner does not immediately register but this was not among them. I felt the surge of euphoria immediately I crossed the line and the fact that it had been the luckiest of breaks for me to be riding the horse did not detract in any way from the way I felt. Afterwards, in the throng of the winners' enclosure, receiving the trophy and talking to the press (this is one occasion when no jockey considers this duty a chore) I wanted the experience to last forever, to bottle all the feelings for posterity. Instead, the Grand Annual Chase and the County Hurdle beckoned and, for once at Cheltenham, I needed to make a conscious effort to get my mind refocused onto riding another race.

Winning the Gold Cup is a career high for any jockey and, if the

Top: Mum and Dad with 70's haircuts - the baby on the left is me
Middle right: Early horsepower, with brother Nick
Middle left: Mum leading up Sea Cargo, a family horse
Above: Dad shows his style in a point-to-point

Above: Three generations of Johnsons pose with Bridge Ash after his win in the Midlands Grand National

Above: My first pony, Tasty - 20 years on, she is still fit and well

Right: Leading up a winner for the first time at the Maisemore point-to-point

Opposite:
Riding at the Weston
Park horse trials,
aged 15

Opposite:
Mum's father, who
sadly died when I was
young

Opposite:
With Corner Boy, the
best horse I did at
David Nicholson's
yard

Top and above: Two views of Stratford racecourse, a generation apart - Dad on Sea Cargo and me on Maggotts Green, upsides Richard Dunwoody

Right: Winning at Haydock on the classy but injury-prone Relkeel

Left: Space Mariner, my first point-to-point winner

Above: A winner for David Nicholson at Aintree, on Splendid

Below: What's Up Boys and Bindaree battle it out in the 2002 National
Bottom: Rusty Bridge winning a hunters chase

Above: Sandybraes wins at Market Rasen

Right: All my fault. Waterberg stood up to win

Above: A rare flat winner at Haydock

Left: More novice chase alarms

Below: A winner at Stratford on Dick the Taxi

Above: Seemed like a good idea ...
messrs Thornton, Aizpuru, Johnson and
McPhail with dyed hair to raise money
for injured colleague Scott Taylor

Right: Rusty Bridge again, this time in
defeat at Stratford

Above: My first Cheltenham festival ride,
on Strong Beau

Right: My first ride over fences for David
Nicholson, on Musthaveaswig

The anatomy of a fall that looks a lot worse than it was. I landed running and the horse, Peachy, was fine after this episode at the last hurdle at Hereford

Practising a flying dismount ...
ejected by the side door in a hurdle
race at Hereford

Above: Proud moments. Receiving congratulations from the Queen Mother after winning the Cheltenham Gold Cup on Looks Like Trouble

Below: More Cheltenham glory, with Colin Smith (second left) and the Duke (centre) after Anzum's win in the Stayers Hurdle

Opposite: Just for once, I look more stylish than A.P.McCoy - and I won the race, at Uttoxeter, on Newton Point

Top: Flagship Uberalles wins the Tingle Creek Chase ...

Above: ... and the Queen Mother Champion Chase ...

Right: ... which led to this celebration ...

Opposite: ... and this presentation

Top and above: What's Up Boys wins a novice chase at Aintree in 2001, but he just failed to win the big one there the following year

Top: Great jockey, great friend. A.P.McCoy

Above: With Zara at a black-tie function in London

Not again! Breaking my right leg at
Newton Abbot, August 2002

peculiarity of the achievement for me was that it came out of the blue, the extra perk of victory came in keeping the ride. Noel had things well mapped out, almost as if he had fully anticipated the Cheltenham victory, and he was soon telling everyone that the horse's next run would be in his native Ireland in November. The race chosen was at Down Royal, just outside Belfast, and it was to be my first visit. The track is in sight of the notorious Maze prison but the management has worked wonders to raise its profile and the turnout of both people and quality horses for their Festival raceday was a vindication of their efforts. Those present saw something special, too, for Looks Like Trouble's performance there was the finest by any horse I have ridden. It is, of course, foolish to compare the great steeplechasers of history but it would have taken a quite extraordinary horse to beat him that day.

I had thought that Mr Mulligan was the best I'd ridden, especially the way he ran when winning the Reynoldstown Chase, but at Down Royal I rode a horse that could fly. At every fence, he took off from a point where other horses would be contemplating one more stride, possibly two. He was jumping houses and, after three or four fences in this style, I virtually left him to it and became an admiring passenger. On some horses, such spectacular jumping would have been scary for the rider but Looks Like Trouble just felt totally happy and in control. He was not jumping big and landing steeply, he was sailing over the fences as if they were hurdles, and landing running every time. Noel had told me before the race that the horse had improved and I'm afraid to say I laughed. He had won the Gold Cup by five lengths last time out - how could he improve on that? But he was right, and that was the first thing I said when I came back to unsaddle. It was as if the Gold Cup had woken him up to the demands of proper racing. At Cheltenham, he went around with the pack, at one stage idling dangerously, but at Down Royal he knew precisely what he was there to do and took a mature, superior pleasure in doing it.

What a dreadful shame that injury intervened at this point. The racing world was still absorbing what it had witnessed, the public agog and the bookmakers busily shortening his odds for a Cheltenham repeat, when poor Noel was confronted with the evidence that every trainer dreads, let alone one with the most exciting horse seen in years. He had tendon trouble, nothing career-threatening but enough for any sensible trainer to call a halt to the programme and think of the longer term. It had taken until the Monday, two days after Down Royal, for the problem to make itself known and although the likelihood is that he did it during the race, it remains possible that he banged the leg in his stable, or on the return journey. We shall never be sure. All I do know for certain is that to have run and jumped as brilliantly as he did, he could not have been feeling any niggles during the race.

The news was devastating for all, from Noel to Tim Collins through the stable staff. It was a bitter pill for me, too. Jockeys do not have to cope with the precarious emotions that come with day-to-day care of horses - one good reason why I shall never be a trainer - but that does not diminish the sense of loss at times like this. If he had stayed sound, I regarded him as a certainty to win the Gold Cup again the following March. I could not imagine what could possibly beat him.

As it turned out, the fall-out from foot-and-mouth disease meant that there was no Gold Cup that year, so in a sense we were spared the extreme frustration of having got him to the race as clear favourite only to see the event abandoned. Noel, who is a marvel at dealing with the press, continued to put a brave face on the situation as the horse recuperated, claiming that a year off was no bad thing, but naturally he knew how much luck was required to bring back such a high-class chaser in the form he had been before the injury. So often, we see trainers nursing horses back and issuing reassuring statements about their work and attitude, only for the first reacquaintance with a racecourse to show a markedly inferior animal.

This did not happen with Looks Like Trouble, though. He made his comeback in January 2002 at Wincanton and, though I had tried my best to hasten my own return from injury, I had to concede to nature and watch Seamus Durack ride him. There are people, I know, who say it was a poor race he won that day and that it proved nothing, but I disagree. I liked the style and attitude of the performance, over a trip way short of his best, and when I was fit enough to go down to Lambourn to school him, and then to ride him in a piece of racecourse work, he felt the same horse I had known before.

Despite so long an absence, he actually went to Cheltenham able to defend his title, won two years earlier, and I was among those who kept the faith and believed him fully capable of doing it. I set out to ride him positively, because he had enjoyed the trailblazing so much at Down Royal, but although he got to the front and kept a fairly uncontested lead for most of the race, I had misgivings at an early stage. He was jumping out to one side, often a sign that a horse is feeling an injury, yet he was travelling so strongly that there was no way I could be sure he was wrong. I thought perhaps it was a mental legacy, that he was simply being careful and favouring one leg. Certainly, there was no evidence to pull him up and when we came down the hill to the second last he still held a narrow lead. It was then, though, that his stride shortened as if he was suddenly weary. Two or three horses, including the impressive winner, Best Mate, swept past on the final turn and although we jumped the last safely enough I knew all was not well and eased him right down, jumping off as soon as he crossed the line.

Walking him back down the course, as the crowd cheered for a new hero, was an odd, empty experience but no jockey has the right to think he will win the Gold Cup more than once. I was sad for Noel and all the work he had put in, and sad for the horse, because this was a desperately inappropriate way for him to finish. I think I knew, in those moments, that he would be retired and I would never get to ride him again, yet Looks Like Trouble showed his character to the very end. Some horses, like some people, are wimps when it comes to any hint of pain but he did not want to limp and by the time I was nearing the unsaddling enclosure I had almost kidded myself that he was not lame at all. He was a brave, proud animal, one of the best I shall ever know.

A.P.McCoy

13.

'Not him again'

T o n y   M c C o y

It was one of his direct predecessors who summed it up best. David Bridgwater is a trainer now but, for a brief spell in the 1990s, he was stable jockey to Martin Pipe. For most, this has been a dream job, a gateway to the title but it just didn't work out for 'Bridgie'. In his final season of riding, he was resigned to the fact that he could no longer compete with the young Irishman who was carrying all before him. Tony McCoy was plainly destined to be a dominant presence in the weighing-room for years to come but, as David said: "It would be much easier to ride against him if you didn't like him."

Time after time, I am asked to tell people how we REALLY get on, the implication being that two such fierce rivals on the course, accustomed to slugging it out alongside each other, are probably at each other's throats in private. Nothing, though, could be further from the truth. It may sound anodyne to those lusting after scandal but the truth is that we have never fallen out, nor felt any need to do so. I usually sit near to him at racing, as we share the same valet and a similar level of seniority, and rather than sharing earnest conversation about rides or horses there is usually plenty of friendly banter between us on a daily basis. I might say I couldn't understand why a certain horse had jumped badly, or ask him what he thought of the quality of a race we had just ridden in, but we would be unlikely to discuss specific riding problems. Perhaps it's the rival cavalry thing; more likely, we each direct such matters to different sets of ears.

I feel we are in a fortunate era, blessed with a generation of very high quality jockeys who also make up into an outstanding group of people. 'A.P.', as he is called by all, is a fine example. He is a very hard opponent on the racecourse but, off duty, he would do anything for you. Sure, there will be jockeys who envy him his position but I know of none who resent him.

This is not to say, of course, that I applaud all his winners without a thought for myself. Human nature rails against that kind of altruism. It frustrates the hell out of me when he is riding winners and I'm not. While I was out with that broken leg, late in 2001, I began to drive myself slowly insane by watching him increase his lead over me, day after day. It is frequently said that the only way I can beat him to the jockeys' title, as things stand, is if he has a similar type of injury and while it is generally true that no jockey wishes bad falls on another, it would be a great deal easier to desire if he was not such a nice bloke.

Shortly after I had returned from injury, I drove to Doncaster to ride what I was convinced would be my first winner back. At the time, Dark'n'Sharp was just what his name suggested - he was unconsidered by many, a Festival dark horse, yet we thought he was sharp enough to go to Cheltenham for the Arkle Chase, the two-mile novices' championship event. He would have won on his fencing debut but for coming down at the last at Huntingdon and now he had only two opponents at Doncaster. I completed the motorway drive cheerfully, certain that this was the day to get me back on the scoreboard. Run the race again now and Dark'n'Sharp would win it every time, for subsequently he finished third at Cheltenham (in a handicap) and won at both Aintree and Ayr. But on that occasion, to my intense disappointment, he was beaten a head by Hit and Run, trained by M.Pipe and ridden by A.P. Everyone told me it was a rousing finish between us, just the sort of duel that had been missing while I was away. I glowered and brooded at the perceived injustice. All those winners he'd ridden in my absence and now he had to take this one from me, too. Life briefly seemed a bitch.

It can, for sure, be more galling for me to lose out to A.P. in a finish than to anyone else. "Not him again, why can't I beat him for once," and similar thoughts rush through my head at such times. It also nags at me that people will inevitably compare us and that win he registers in a head-to-head with me will further fuel the possibility of owners or trainers thinking they might have won with A.P. on board. On the other hand, if McCoy beats you it is much easier to make the comforting assumption that your horse just wasn't good enough. It's not so easy to shelter behind such reasoning when you have lost out to some unco-ordinated amateur.

It is never a nice feeling to sense him cruising alongside you, yet even if he is pushing desperately with three to jump you cannot relax, because you know for certain that he will never give up. I like to think we are similar in that way - maybe we are both just too thick to recognise defeat and that's why we keep pushing and shoving for so long. Certainly, we share the mentality that, if we cannot win, second is better than third, and so on.

I first recall meeting Anthony, as he was initially known, one autumn afternoon at Stratford. He had just arrived in England after learning the ropes under Jim Bolger in Ireland and my first emotion was doubtless that he simply added to the number of Irishmen outnumbering we home-breds in the weighing-room. I do remember, though, being struck by how painfully skinny he looked, the scrawny body somehow disproportionate to his height. I made a mental note that he might struggle with his weight sooner rather than later.

I was correct, of course, but it has not stopped him - in two senses. He still rides winners at a faster rate than any jockey in history and he still has a desperately bad diet. It is not quite as bad as it used to be, when his intake seemed to consist of Coca-Cola, Kit-Kats and fast-food. He has cut out the burgers now, and gone easy on the chips, but he still consumes more Kit-Kats than anyone I know and - as a teetotaller - drinks vast quantities of Coke.

I am not in a position to give anyone grief about their diet, as I rebel against the notion of a lettuce-leaf discipline and eat anything put in front of me. Ours is a job that uses up a great deal of energy and we all need to replace it somehow. My greatest advantage, though, is having no weight problem, no need for remorse or panic after an extravagant meal. A.P. is fighting a constant battle with the scales and has to deal with the situation as he sees fit. On occasion, this will involve him not eating (well, other than the odd Kit-Kat) for up to three days. Some days, if he is straining to meet a light weight, he can certainly look worryingly drawn and grey when he arrives at racing but you may rest assured that he will have a very different pallor if he goes home with a couple of winners. From personal experience, I can recall going racing feeling awful, picking up an unexpected win and suddenly feeling on top of the world. The flipside is no less applicable - many times I have driven to a meeting without a care in the world, suffered a run of reversals and returned home feeling sick and tired.

One area in which Tony does have the advantage over me is that he can lie in his bed longer in the morning. Other than the handful of times each year (generally early-season and pre-Cheltenham) when he is required to go to Martin Pipe's yard for a schooling session, riding-out is not on his agenda. Very few jump jockeys can get away with this undoubted privilege and there can be no question that it helps A.P. conserve his energy for the racecourse.

As he also has Gee Armytage, his personal assistant, on hand to answer the phone, organise his diary and generally run his life, the only thing he actually has to do is turn up and ride. I'm sure a lot of jockeys would love to be in that position and there have been many midwinter mornings, crawling out of bed before dawn for the unattractive prospect of schooling some ignorant creatures in pouring rain, when I would have swapped places with him like a shot. When I view it rationally, though, I recognise that I quite enjoy riding out and there is no doubt that I get some long-term benefits from it, not just in keeping a variety of trainers happy and tuned in to my presence but also in building up a store of knowledge about their horses and earning the reassurance that comes from having schooled them myself when they go to the racecourse. With all that said, though, McCoy is one lucky man to be able to laze around until mid-morning day after day.

Many have tried to analyse his riding and pass judgement on what it is that makes him one of the best there has ever been. Clearly, it is a combination of physical, technical and mental attributes that creates his unique mix but the most compelling feature, to my eye, is that he keeps a horse's momentum going better than anyone I've seen. No matter the standard of the horse, it will be running to its optimum speed and rhythm for as long as A.P. is on board.

Nowadays, he manages to achieve this without being anything like as aggressive early in a race as he once was, a refinement that has not harmed his riding and has allowed him to remain freer of suspensions.

The whip issue will never be cut-and-dried, because for every jockey convinced it was only that final crack that empowered his horse to win there will be someone out there condemning it as needless abuse - the line is so fine that no regulation can adequately cover the situation. My riding with the stick has improved with maturity, as it should in all jockeys, but both A.P. and I will still have days when we overstep the mark in search of a winner. It can, of course, be expensive in terms of revenue and winners, and I reckon that getting through a season without suspensions can, by comparison with any given year in the past, gain me 20 winners. I will never accept that either of us abuses a horse, though, and one issue on which we talk quite frequently is the sense of grievance that comes from acquiring a whip ban through giving everything to win a race, while some horse trailing at the back of the field has been unnecessarily hit four or five times and the stewards have turned a blind eye. Sometimes, we both feel that stewards should be looking at races in a different way, taking a less punitive view of those involved in a close finish and being more concerned with the gratuitous use of the whip that can often be seen among the also-rans.

This sort of whip use is most evident among young riders desperate to make an impression. All of them, of course, want to be like A.P. but there are many who go the wrong way about it. One of McCoy's trademarks is taking a race by the scruff of the neck with the bulldozing, front-running he so often attempts on a Pipe horse. Watch him in action, even on an average horse from the yard, and you can be fooled into thinking he just goes flat out from flagfall, kicking into every obstacle. It is, of course, a bit more scientific than that and Tony knows that these are extremely fit horses placed in a race they can win and sure to sustain the pace he is setting. Week after week, though, I watch bright-eyed young jockeys trying to imitate A.P. on hopelessly inadequate horses - they set off too fast, go long at every hurdle and either end up on the floor or tailing off with a mile to run having distressed and disillusioned their horse in the process.

It can be argued, then, that A.P. unwittingly sets a detrimental example to younger jockeys in this respect. In my view, the same may be said about his demeanour at the Cheltenham Festival in 2002, though in this instance he was more in control of the impression he was giving. His depression following the death of Valiramix in the Champion Hurdle was, at first, understandable. The longer it went on, though, and the more overt his brooding became, the more he lost sympathy. I ended up feeling disappointed by him but hopeful that he would learn something from it.

The weighing-room was certainly an interesting place that week. During Cheltenham, it always is, as some jockeys experience the unrivalled highs of Festival success while others fret over their dashed dreams. I was lucky in 2002 but, unusually, neither Mick Fitzgerald nor Norman Williamson rode a winner. Their disappointment was obvious but it was kept in control, not least by the far greater misfortunes of certain colleagues. Adrian Maguire was in hospital having his broken neck operated upon, while Tony Dobbin rode only reluctantly after the shattering blow of losing his brother in a car crash. The winner he did ride on the opening day meant nothing to him and, following a fall on the Wednesday, he went home on Gold Cup morning, relieved to be alone with his thoughts. He said that riding was just a job and that there were more important things to attend to - he was right, too. No matter how smitten we are by our lifestyle and our racing world, it should not rule anyone's life.

Set against such events, even the death of a very fine horse has to be put in perspective. Tony failed to do that and I felt he reacted disproportionately. Of course, it was terribly disappointing for him - that goes without saying. Valiramix had been challenging for favouritism in the Champion Hurdle and, once Istabraq had been pulled-up with the race barely underway, he was the most likely winner. Turning down the hill, he was travelling so well that A.P. must have begun to believe it was his race. For the horse to fall fatally on the flat at such a critical point in a championship race is devastating for a jockey and it would be hypocritical for me to say otherwise. I felt for Tony in the immediate aftermath. I also believed he was being unduly self-critical in blaming himself because, in my opinion, Valiramix did not clip heels with another horse but simply broke his shoulder freakishly. It was a horrible thing to happen.

He sat desolately in the weighing-room between rides for the rest of that day and, long after racing, was still statuesque in his corner, though with a towel draped over his head. There was no point in in trying to bring him around or reason with him and I think everyone just hoped he would have recovered his poise the next day. But he hadn't. I got a call asking me to fill in for him as guest on 'The Morning Line', which was indicative of his unaltered mood, and he continued in what can only be described as a silent sulk, that day and the next. Even a winner - following an admittedly infuriating sequence of seconds - lifted the depression only temporarily.

I know I have raged on the bad days. I'm not a good loser and, when an apparent conspiracy of a day is over, I've gone home and refused to speak, sulking like a little boy. Without exception, though, I have managed to get up the following day and start again. In this job, I think that is essential. In hindsight, I also learnt a great deal about myself during the lengthy inactivity caused by my broken leg. I remember one day in particular, sat at home with 'Shav' Aizpuru, saying I had realised so much more clearly why I had wanted to be a jockey and how lucky I was in the way I lived my life and the horses I could ride. Absence, certainly, had made me heart very much fonder and my mind much clearer. It was an education, one that I hope I can remember and put to good use.

I would honestly hate for Tony to have to go through such an injury in order to find that perspective, which is why I hope the events at Cheltenham were enough, in themselves, to have made him think seriously about the way he behaved. Perhaps part of the problem was that he has been so accustomed to things going right. For any other jockey, riding a winner and five seconds at the Cheltenham Festival would have been fantastic but it did not satisfy him and his grief over the loss of one of his best horses made his gloom almost unbearable. We all get upset when horses die, especially good ones, but it is part of a jockey's job to be realistic about such things and never to take out the upset on other people.

I know he was aware that people were surprised and even offended by him that week and I think he was genuinely regretful about upsetting them. It would not have been his way to do that on purpose but, as a man at the top of his profession, he should know he is in the goldfish bowl in Cheltenham week, subject to the closest of scrutiny. Thankfully, come the end of the week he was back in the form we all know best, a gentleman in the weighing-room, a grafter on the racecourse and a great one for a night out.

Forget the fact that he never touches a drop of alcohol - it is no such of prudishness, he has just found he hates the taste. If there is a party in the offing, A.P. will be there, probably longer than most. For the sake of racing, I hope the same is true of his career. For my own selfish sake, I wonder if he might just see his way clear to retiring next season?

Florida Pearl

14.

A measure of respect
F l o r i d a   P e a r l

British racing is full of Irish jockeys, some of whom came here as lads while others travelled across only after making a reputation in their homeland. There are times, as an Englishman, when I feel thoroughly outnumbered in the weighing-room and it is only natural that, when riding opportunities in Ireland arise, the native Irishmen tend to be favoured. It was for this, as much as for any other reason, that I felt a special sense of pride at being asked to ride Florida Pearl during February of 2001. To be allowed to ride the best steeplechaser in the country, indeed a horse that has attained folk-hero status, was to me a sign of acceptance in Ireland, and gave me such a sense of pride. The fact that I managed to win on him was a gratifying bonus.

The chance came quite unexpectedly. Florida Pearl has had a variety of jockeys during his career - a trend that has continued since - but Ruby Walsh, as stable jockey to the trainer Willie Mullins, had first claim on him that season and had been on board when he ran a perfectly respectable second behind First Gold in the King George VI Chase. Unfortunately for Ruby, he picked up an injury the day before the Irish Hennessy Gold Cup was due to be run at Leopardstown. With Paul Carberry, another to have won on the horse, also out with a broken leg, the connections had to cast around for somebody new. Greatly to my surprise, they came to me.

It was a Saturday evening and I had just returned home from the afternoon's racing when Dave Roberts rang with the news. I was flattered but also taken aback, having assumed that an Irish jockey would get the call, but I now had to get myself organised with flights from Birmingham to Dublin. There are jockeys who do this route almost every Sunday, taking advantage of the fact that the Irish race on a day that is still usually free of racing in Britain during the winter. Others will go over for midweek Irish meetings when the opportunity arises. Norman Williamson is the prime example and, these days, he virtually splits his time between the countries and rides as much for Edward O'Grady, who trains down in Co.Tipperary, as he does for his British trainers. It works well for Norman, especially as he has accepted that he will never be champion jockey in Britain, but my priorities are to ride as many winners as possible on my home courses. Given the choice of one decent ride in Ireland or four with a chance at Sedgefield, I would choose Sedgefield every time. Because of that, I have still not ridden on many Irish courses and even Leopardstown, south-east of Dublin, was new to me.

So, too, was Willie Mullins. I knew of him as an ex-jockey who had done marvellously well since following his father, Paddy, into the training ranks, but apart from saying hello to each other at the races we had barely had cause to speak. I liked his manner from the start - he is a gentleman but sharp with it, and it was clear that he knew his own mind. Having said that, he did not try to tie me down with any restrictive orders, allowing me to ride Florida Pearl the way the race dictated I should.

In December of that year, while I was laid up with my broken leg, Adrian Maguire was showered with well-merited praise for the positive ride he gave Florida Pearl when he beat Best Mate and Bacchanal in the King George. Many, it seemed, were surprised that he responded so well to such tactics, yet in effect I had done exactly the same thing on him at Leopardstown, and he plainly loved it. We led virtually throughout the second circuit and his bold jumping told me everything I needed to know about his frame of mind. He was here to try and become only the second horse in history to win this Irish landmark race three times, and there seemed no chance of him being denied.

The ground was heavy but Leopardstown, I discovered, is not an especially stiff track and Florida motored around it like a Bentley until the last 50 yards, when it was as if the engine had stalled. He stopped almost to a walk and had only two lengths to spare at the line from his unfancied stable companion, Alexander Banquet. The others, who included Commanche Court and Native Upmanship, were a very long way adrift and I always thought I would hold on to win but I had to resort to a great deal more visible effort than had seemed likely. The winning margin did no justice to the superiority of my horse for all but that final stretch of the race, yet in tying up as he did he helped me to understand him better.

He had felt the real deal that day, travelling smoothly and jumping with an easy fluency you rarely come across. He did everything with such authority that I could well see why the Irish had fallen in love with him and why he is so much the apple of his trainer's eye that he has a lifesize wire sculpture of the horse in his back garden. Now, though, I had also seen at first hand his achilles heel of stamina. When the ground is bad, the three-mile trip is just beyond his optimum. Even when it rides good, three-and-a-quarter round Cheltenham, the Gold Cup trip, has consistently stretched his resources to breaking point. What a frustration, in some ways, to have a horse of such inordinate ability, yet to find himself unable to impose it on the race by which all the great staying steeplechasers have to be judged. Yet could anyone really complain about the omissions in Florida Pearl's career, when he has spent it all on the top shelf of jump racing and conquered virtually everything bar the Gold Cup?

Like every other horse, though, he is subject to the odd, inexplicable bad day and I am afraid he had one of them on the only other occasion I had the privilege of riding him. There was no Cheltenham that year, due to foot-and-mouth, and Willie decided not to send him to Aintree, either. Instead, he kept him back for the grade one race that would normally be run at the Punchestown Festival and known as the Heineken Gold Cup. That season, the meeting was switched to Fairyhouse but it attracted a predictably small but elite field of Irish chasers and Florida Pearl was sent off as odds-on favourite. Strictly on form, it was difficult to argue with the bookmakers and I certainly went there feeling confident that a repeat of the Leopardstown run would be more than enough to ensure victory. For whatever reason, however, he did not run within a stone of that form, nor even jump with the same vigour. The race was won by an outsider, in Moscow Express, and we just about held on to second spot ahead of Dorans Pride. Willie wondered whether he was just short of a gallop, as foot-and-mouth had impeded his preparations, but to me he did not even feel the same horse that had run at Leopardstown.

This was the day I learned what a nice bunch of people are around the horse. Quite apart from the trainer, who was more inclined to blame himself than anyone else, Florida has two charming owners in Archie and Violet O'Leary. Archie is actually a rugby fan by choice and he first bought a horse or two just for a little fun between internationals at Lansdowne Road. A horse like this one, though, can change your outlook on life and he has since bought several more. They seem model owners to me, delighted to be at the races, intent on having fun and never inclined to complain. If only the entire breed was like that.

Having had the chance to get to know Florida Pearl, however briefly, I find I follow his career more closely now. In the 2001-2 season, he found Kempton's sharp three miles on goodish ground right up his street but in the Gold Cup at Cheltenham he turned in another performance like the Fairyhouse run with me, never carrying Conor O'Dwyer at all. Although I was fit by then, Willie had not offered me the ride and I would not have expected him to do so. Adrian would obviously have ridden him but for injury, by which time I was fully committed to Looks Like Trouble. At Aintree, for the Martell Cup, Barry Geraghty became another new jockey for Florida and, once again, he responded well to a change of pilot, giving a brilliant exhibition round and actually quickening up between the last two flights. It was good ground again that day, and a sharp track - when he gets such conditions, he can look virtually unbeatable.

I am sure the Gold Cup keeps Willie awake at nights and I do know he has not given up hope of winning it with the horse. To my mind, though, he will need very quick ground at Cheltenham to get home, and even then I would not be confident. That last quarter-mile, all uphill, seems to find him out with his petrol gauge on empty, and I cannot see why that should change now. As Cheltenham is such a demanding track, his best chance there would be if they created a two-and-a-half mile championship race, which is apparently on the cards if and when the Festival extends to a fourth day. By then, I am afraid, Florida Pearl's great career will be over.

Failing to win a Gold Cup, though, should not diminish his other achievements and I think it is terribly sad that he has never quite received his due credit. This is one of the very best horses I have ridden or seen during my time, so good I would compare him to the brilliant One Man, the grey who won two King George's but also found the Gold Cup hill beyond him more than once. One Man was quick enough to come back to two miles and win a Champion Chase in 1998 and the same route has often been mooted for Florida Pearl, though I would be surprised if he took it.

The fact is that the horse has won ten grade one races, starting with a Cheltenham champion bumper when he was having only the second run of his life. The day that One Man won the Champion Chase, Florida Pearl beat the Duke's Escartefigue in the Sun Alliance Chase, so it is not as if he has an a version to Cheltenham itself. He has never competed below the highest level, never been given an easy run, yet year after year he has come up with more glittering victories. I would love the chance to ride him again but, if it never comes, I shall still treasure the memory. It was not just that I got to ride one of the best horses of my lifetime, it was the vote of confidence from Ireland that meant so much.

Flagship Uberalles

15.
Brotherly standards
Flagship Uberalles

Viking Flagship was one of the best two-mile chasers for many years, a titan of his generation and a hero to all of us working at David Nicholson's yard, not least to the trainer himself. There was a strange symmetry to the fact that this wonderful horse was retired in March of 1998, a month before I first came across the half-brother who was to emulate him. I only rode Viking Flagship in the last year of his great career but I've been luckier with Flagship Uberalles. My greatest good fortune, though, is that I am the one jockey who has had the chance to compare them at the closest quarters.

My first ride on the elder brother was a disappointment. It was the April meeting at Cheltenham in 1997 and he was probably feeling the effects of a hard season as he trailed in third of four behind Strong Promise. The following season, I won on him twice, including first time out in the Haldon Gold Cup, in which Adrian Maguire had chosen to partner the stable's better fancied Mulligan. I kept the ride when he won the Castleford Chase at Wetherby over Christmas but Adrian was back for his farewell. He had run at six successive Cheltenham Festivals and this was his fifth Queen

Mother Champion Chase, including two wins. It was the right stage for his exit and it was just a shame he could finish only fifth. At 11 years old, though, he owed none of us anything, and had left all racing followers with a host of great memories.

The Duke enjoyed sending horses to the Punchestown Festival in April but, that year, it was so curtailed by bad weather that they ended up running four grade one races on the same day. Among them was a championship four-year-old race that we managed to win with Zafarabad. It was well-merited reward for a horse that had gone into the Triumph Hurdle at Cheltenham as favourite but finished only fourth, yet in hindsight the most significant aspect of a thrilling race was that the horse placed third - ridden by A.P.McCoy and beaten only two necks - was Flagship Uberalles. The last foal produced by Fourth Degree, he was trained in Co. Waterford then, by P.J.Flynn, and had won a couple of juvenile events at Navan and Limerick, but pretty soon afterwards he was making the first of several moves that were to await him in an eventful, nomadic career.

Paul Nicholls was the first of his British-based trainers and he wasted no time sending him over fences. He won his first novice chase at Exeter in December of that year, while still a four-year-old, and ended up winning the Arkle Chase at Cheltenham and the grade one novice event at Aintree. He seemed to have everything - not least youth - on his side and was clearly going to be a leading fancy for the following year's Champion Chase, an impression he reinforced by beating most of his main rivals twice at the start of the 1999-2000 season. On the big day itself, however, he could finish only third behind that stirring duel between Edredon Bleu and Direct Route. The ground was probably too fast for him but he was then beaten at both Aintree and Ayr before being removed from the Nicholls yard and rehoused in Lambourn with Noel Chance.

As Noel had just won the Gold Cup with Looks Like Trouble, he had never been more fashionable and there were those in the game who felt he now had the two best steeplechasers in the country in his yard. To others, though, Flagship still had something to prove. Up to this point, I had just been an interested observer of his career but when Noel asked me to ride Flagship, as well as Looks Like Trouble, I felt a very privileged man. The luck had worn a shade thinner by the time I actually came to ride Flagship, as Looks Like Trouble had suffered the injury that was to blight and ultimately end his career, but the Tingle Creek Chase in December was enough to convince me that I now had the ride on potentially the best two-miler around.

The race was transferred to Cheltenham that year, as Sandown was having its winter of discontent with constant waterlogging problems. Edredon Bleu was absent but the rest of the speed machines of steeplechasing were all present and correct and, to be honest, my horse slaughtered them. I was not confident of such an outcome all the way round, though. For the first mile, which was run at a terrific gallop, he didn't carry me as easily as I had imagined he would. This was my first inkling that pace was not actually his greatest asset. When the others were tiring, he came forging into his own and he ran right away from them to win by 11 lengths. Just as had happened the previous year after this very race, he was then promoted to favouritism for the Champion Chase, yet once again it was not to be. This time, it was hardly his fault, as the race did not even take place due to foot-and-mouth, but by spring he had blotted his copybook again with a below-par run at Newbury. The opposition in the Game Spirit Chase was not that strong and I thought he would definitely win, but he did not handle the sticky ground and came back lame.

This was his second injury of what was becoming a frustrating season. Earlier, he had suffered an overreach which prevented Noel from implementing a plan to run him in the King George at Kempton. In hindsight, it would have been very interesting to see how he coped with the sharp three miles, though as the race came less than three weeks after his Cheltenham win, it would almost certainly have been too soon.

After further defeats, at Aintree and Sandown, Noel became the third trainer to lose the horse, in his case after a single season. Plenty of eyebrows were raised at this, the common remark being that the next trainer to be sent Flagship would be receiving something of a poisoned chalice. Naturally, I had to wonder if this latest switch would bring with it a change of jockey but I was fortunate again. Philip Hobbs was the newly nominated trainer, which pretty much guaranteed that I would be keeping the ride.

Flagship's owners are an American couple, Elizabeth Gutner and Michael Krysztofiak, who have not received the kindest of press over their rapid rotation of trainers, something that happens only rarely with high profile horses. Their reasons are their own but it is every owner's entitlement to employ who he wants, both to train and to ride. I can only speak as a jockey and my dealings with them have been unfailingly civil. So far as I am aware, in fact, they have never had a problem over the riding of the horse - Joe Tizzard did nothing wrong in the two seasons he rode Flagship for Paul Nicholls and the owners still get along well with him. I am the only other jockey to have ridden Flagship on a regular basis and they have never got upset with me, or in my company, even after disappointing defeats. Before a race, they are very confident owners - they want to win and are not ashamed to say so - but in my experience they have accepted all results well. Another thing I would say in their favour is that they give the impression that the health of their horses is of primary importance. They had another horse that got injured at Aintree a couple of years ago and subsequently invested both time and money in the treatment needed for his recovery.

With that said, I am sure it was uppermost in Philip's mind that he was going to be under some scrutiny after the horse had been removed from two top trainers. His solution was very shrewd. On all the evidence, Flagship was a far better horse when fresh than later in a busy season, so Philip proposed that he should have only two targets for the season and, effectively, come fresh to both of them. Some owners, intent on watching their horses run as frequently as possible, would have raised objections but I understand the idea went down well and Flagship was duly pencilled in for the Tingle Creek, which he was trying to win for a third successive year, and the Champion Chase. There was a gap between races of more than four months, in which Philip could freshen up the horse to the point of kidding him that he was starting another new season.

The plan could hardly have been better executed, other than from the selfish viewpoint of his jockey. I was still on crutches when he won the Tingle Creek again and it was one of the most frustrating days of my three-month lay-off. The owners were loyal, though, promising I would have the ride back at Cheltenham, and this time he did not fluff his lines. The ground was on the soft side, which brought his undoubted stamina into play and, simultaneously, blunted the speed of the reigning champion, Edredon Bleu. By now, too, I was familiar with the notion that Flagship might appear to be labouring through the first half of the race, so it did not unduly concern me when the hectic pace of the early stages was too much for him. I had to work hard to keep him in contention but it is much easier to push a horse that has the will and the energy to give more than one that is simply at the end of its tether. I relied on my confidence that the leaders must come back to me, such had been the early pace, and eventually they did. Cenkos had run the race of his life but he began to tie up at the second last and my horse was not stopping. I knew, coming to the last, that he only had to jump it to win.

He did run once more, at Sandown Park's finale meeting, and he had been in such good form after Cheltenham that there was nothing to indicate he should not. In retrospect, we were probably fooled, as I recalled Noel Chance telling me he had seemed an improved horse at home after winning the Tingle Creek - yet on the track, he had definitely taken some sharp steps backwards. As it was the last day of a light season, no damage was done by the run at Sandown but he was beaten, nonetheless, Cenkos turning the tables in quite remarkable fashion considering he had made the marathon trip for a race in Japan after Cheltenham.

That result could not alter the fact that Flagship was the two-mile champion of 2002 and it reflected great credit on the methods of the Hobbs yard. It is a very happy, relaxed operation down near Minehead and the environment of the converted farm (formerly run by Philip's father), with the sea close at hand, seems to make for contented horses. They do not go short of work - the gallop there is so stiff I would certainly not fancy running up it three times in a morning - but the programme never seems to be pressurised and benefits from a sense of variety. Flagship, who has had his share of physical problems, was taken regularly down to the beach as he built up to Cheltenham and Philip said he seemed to enjoy going in the sea.

Though he is still only eight, Flagship has had quite a career already, what with four different trainers and a good few setbacks mixed in with the big wins. He has been operating at top level for a long time and, as a horse has an optimum mileage, it will increasingly be a matter of conserving his energies for the big days. Where they will be, it remains to be seen but there is a real possibility that the King George VI Chase option will be revisited. I am pretty sure Flagship will never be a Cheltenham Gold Cup horse but the three miles round Kempton could be within his range. If it is, all manner of routes are open to us. The priority, though, is to keep him happy and healthy for as long as possible.

16.

A week in the life of a jump jockey

Alan Lee: No two weeks are exactly alike for a jump jockey, yet most fall into a comparable pattern of unsocial work schedules, too many hours on the road and the physically intense and mentally draining challenge of race-riding six days a week. Often, hopes will be raised too high and summarily dashed; occasionally, a day of no promise brings unimagined rewards. Only the racing itself, of course, is carried out in the spotlight of spectator scrutiny and daily television coverage. There is a lot more to a jockey's job, though, as the diary of a sample week in Richard Johnson's life, shortly after his return from a broken leg, will show.

SUNDAY

It is February, it is cold and dark. The alarm has not woken me, which means it must be Sunday and there is no reason to get out of bed. Bliss. Despite the industrious impression created by endless willing (generally) appearances at training yards shortly after dawn, I like my bed and go through daily agonies of resentment at having to leave it at ungodly hours. Sundays are special, jealously guarded treats. I will ride out occasionally (if my mother needs some help at her yard, the bonus is getting a good Sunday lunch thrown in) but usually only if one of my regular trainers wants a forthcoming runner schooled. Always best not to let any other jockey get on board and make an impression. My preference, though, is to take the morning off and indulge in a luxurious lie-in. It just might be a recuperative one, too, because Saturday is the one night of the week in the busy season (say, October to April) when I do go out and have a few drinks.

My principal rival, A.P.McCoy, does not drink alcohol at all. One of his most famous predecessors, John Francome, was equally abstemious. In both cases, though, they stay off the stuff because they don't like it, rather than through any moral or professional high ground. I make no such claims. I enjoy a social drink and, while I am far from being a connoisseur, I know what I like, which does not include bitter or lager. If I was going to drink pints, cider would be the choice - as befits a Herefordshire boy - but, being only small, I can't hold much anyway. Vodka, with mixers, is my main tipple and, depending on the company, I would have red wine at a nice dinner party.

Most Saturday nights are more casual than that. We have a good crowd of racing folk in the Cotswolds and the mobile phones are usually busy after racing to organise a rendezvous. Last night, it was The Plough, the pub in the dip beneath Jackdaws Castle. A lot of us worked there, at one time or another, and old habits die hard. It's also a good pub, with a genuine racing atmosphere - something we unwittingly hanker after, even when off duty. Food usually enters the equation at some point and Zara and I used to go to the Fosse Manor Hotel a lot - partly to do with my love of rare steaks, which they do especially well. It's also local and, after a busy week darting around the country, that means a lot.

No hangover this morning but that didn't prevent me lingering under the duvet until an hour when I have normally ridden out at least one lot. There's something very satisfying about that. Light, leisurely breakfast, then a chat on the phone to Dave Roberts, my agent, to get some idea where I'm going this week. Tomorrow is Fontwell, for just one ride. I've not been back long from my broken leg and if things are a little quiet, that is largely calculating - plenty of big meetings to come later in the season.

My weight is fine, so a traditional Sunday lunch is a must. It probably has something to do with my country upbringing. Back home by mid afternoon and laze around, seeking to do as little as possible. There is a football match on TV but I don't give it full attention. It's not that I dislike the game but, unlike Warren and A.P. among others, I don't support a club so I never get especially excited. I take more interest in watching a player I have met (some footballers now own horses and I've shared a studio with a few others on programmes like 'Question of Sport') but I save most of my footballing enthusiasm for the five-a-side games we play most weeks through the winter. They usually take place after a local race meeting, a group of us gathering at the indoor school we use for the purpose. Shav Aizpuru is the best player among the Cotswold jockeys but it is probably a good job he never got really good at the game - race callers have quite enough trouble with his name, I dread to think what the football commentators would make of it. Me? I run around for an hour like a headless chicken. Good for the fitness, though.

Unless we are out at a function, Sunday nights in winter-time are invariably spent quietly at home. It may sound boringly domesticated but I really enjoy a switched-off day like this. Tonight, I'm in bed by 10pm. I need my eight hours' sleep if I can get it.

MONDAY

I set my alarm to go off 15 minutes before I am due to leave. This may sound like cutting it dangerously fine but I have the routine off to a fine art. I listen to the jangling bell, pull a face and keep one eye on the clock while snoozing away the next nine minutes, leaving myself six to brush my teeth, drag on some clothes (sometimes pre-prepared, usually not), collect my mobile phone and wallet and stumble out to the car. If I am only going up the road, to ride work for Richard Phillips, I am actually likelier to get the timing wrong and turn up late. This morning, though, it is off to Barbury Castle, near Malvern, to school for Alan King. Alan loves getting his horses out at first light (sometimes before in deep midwinter), so the alarm bell rings for me at 5.30am and I rise feeling Monday-morningish, grumpy and uncommunicative.

Although I am going straight on to Fontwell, I don't need to pack any gear. My racing bag - containing saddles, helmet and body protector - is already in the boot, where it lives. The course valets take all the smaller stuff, along with breeches and boots. Racing boots are made-to-measure and cost about £140 for a decent pair, which should last two or three years even if I'm riding 1,000 races a year. Compare that with the cost of a pair of trainers and it seems decent value. I've got four pairs, which may seem excessive until you consider the spread of our racecourses. I leave one pair with Steve Charlton, the valet who looks after me when I ride in the north. Chris Maude, recently retired from riding, is now my main southern valet and he keeps two lots of gear, while another southern valet, Pat Taylor, keeps a fourth set for me in case Chris is elsewhere on the busiest of racedays.

That's the kit sorted out. I still have to get myself to the races, which is not quite the slumbering pleasure it was during the period when I had a driver. In a full season (one in which I don't break my leg) my car will cover about 80,000 miles, many of them first thing in the morning. I had a girl called Rachel at the wheel for 18 months and, as she quickly proved she knew the best routes to all the tracks, I trusted her completely. So much so that I would get in the car in the mornings and fall straight back to sleep. I still have the pillow in the back that helped me grab the extra 40 minutes' shuteye each day. Sadly, it is now redundant. I'll get by for the rest of this season but when things get busy again in the autumn I shall look for another driver - it does a lot for quality of life in this job.

No jockey can afford to break down - owners and trainers tend to lack understanding of such mishaps - so a good car is important. It is also a vicious circle. The more winners you ride, the better the car you can afford but the likelier you are to get one sponsored. Recently, I got a great deal with Jaguar, who are obligingly replacing my car each time it clocks up 30,000 miles - that's roughly three new cars a year. They are smart, comfortable, quick and I am filling up with petrol, a mile from Barbury Castle, almost before it is properly light.

In the garage I bump into Robert Thornton, commonly known as 'Chocolate' for obvious reasons. Another Cotswold jock, he grew up with me at Jackdaws Castle and is now stable jockey to Kim Bailey. Alan King was for some years assistant trainer to David Nicholson and has remained loyal to the jockeys he knows best - both of us are heading for the schooling session. 'Choc' is pleased to see me. He has just filled up with petrol and realised he has left his wallet at home. That's his story, anyway. Am I a mug to fall for it?

Alan is emerging from his office as we pull in. The yard is approached through Ministry of Defence land, which looks unpromising, but it's a lovely spot when you get there. The sun is up now and my horse head has taken over - I love schooling sessions, especially for trainers I trust, and I start to look forward to the day. Alan, a Scotsman, was one of the lads at the Duke's, always good fun to be around. Now that he has the responsibilities of a trainer he has to be a bit more aloof and, occasionally, he will show the frayed edges that come with responsibility. If the signs are there, I just steer clear and keep my head down. This morning, he barks at one of his lads for being late and curses loudly when Ollie McPhail (another Nicholson refugee) has an unusually heavy fall while schooling. No damage to Ollie, and Alan will know the horse might even benefit from it. Nobody, man or beast, wants to fall but sometimes, if it happens on the schooling ground, it can just help to sharpen up a horse.

After we've schooled some of the imminent runners out on the grass, we return to Alan's playpen - a tiny sand paddock with room for one baby brush fence down each side and a line of logs up through the middle. This is where the young horses are educated and, this morning, I am put on one that has never left the ground before. Cheltenham is barely a fortnight away and a sane jockeys will be taking some precautions to maintain fitness for the biggest week of the year, but the job goes on and you cannot wrap yourself in cotton wool.

I enjoy the process, anyway; there is a real sense of fulfilment in teaching a horse to lift his feet, giving him confidence to do it over ever larger obstacles until he is fluent.

The vocal cabaret, as ever at Barbury, was provided by David Barker. A Liverpudlian, predictably known to all as 'Scouse', he was my appointed minder when I first arrived at Jackdaws. 'The Duke' called him over and told him he was looking after me for a week, showing me the ropes. Well, 'Scouse' did three horses at the time and I ended up mucking out two of them, brushing at least one, picking the feet of them all and doing their feed. 'Scouse' was also good enough to organise my initiation ceremonies, described in painful detail elsewhere. For all that, he is a lovely bloke who gets things done the right way around a racing yard but has the sense of humour to break the ice in any company. He left the Duke's suddenly one year and went to New Zealand to work but I am glad to see him back. Mind you, he is still constantly telling me what's wrong with my riding, despite the fact that he was one of the worst riders ever to set foot in a racing stable before he wisely gave up and attended to other duties.

By 11am, I'd drunk a cup of tea and was on the road to Fontwell. Five minutes after setting off, the mobile phone beeped with a call from Dave Roberts. I sometimes think he must have a tracker device on one of his jockeys, so he knows when to phone. When I started back after injury, we agreed between us that, at least until Cheltenham, I would ride only for my four main trainers unless any obviously attractive spares were offered. In other words, there is no point in taking a ride with no obvious chance just to pocket the fee. As I head south, we discuss options for the remainder of this week. He's got me a ride at Sedgefield tomorrow and it isn't for any of my regular yards but for Oliver Sherwood. Dave says it should win and that is good enough for me - I'd go to Perth for one if he gave me the right encouragement. On Wednesday, I am reluctantly giving up a good ride for Alan King at Doncaster and taking a few at Ludlow. Beyond that, we're not sure.

It takes a little over an hour to the track in West Sussex and I'm there almost two hours before the first, but the car park is already busy. This is one of their best day's racing of the year, with a valuable handicap hurdle the feature event. Fontwell, though, draws a decent crowd even for moderate cards. My one ride is Village King, a real character who is capable of winning on the bridle or tailing himself off at halfway. His race is not until 3.30, so I've got plenty of time to think about it.

Some jockeys head straight for the sauna when they get to the races early. I try to avoid it and, touch wood, I'm lucky enough with my weight to do so most of the time. I don't think anyone actually likes using them but they are a necessity of the job - even for me on occasions. Today, though, I sit back, read the paper and catch up on the gossip of the weighing-room, which is always at its best after the weekend. Inspect the food, eat a ham roll - about as good as it gets here - and then, after a leisurely shave and change into riding gear, it's time for the sports.

I went down to the last fence to watch the novice chase and grinned mischievously at A.P.McCoy being touched off on a 1-2 shot. Back in the weighing-room, he simmered quietly about it, which is normally his way and mine after an unexpected reversal. Some jockeys can be more volatile about it - notable among them the man who beat him today, Timmy Murphy. I probably had my angriest scrap on a racecourse with Timmy, in a 20-runner handicap hurdle at Warwick. With that many runners there will always be some scrimmaging and it was quite early in the race when Timmy shouted to me for room, but I was hemmed in myself and couldn't move. He thought I had deliberately kept him out and, when he came outside me later in the race he leant into me and squeezed me up against the rail. It was out of order and some heated words were exchanged between us. But it never came to blows and it was all forgotten the next day. The truth is that we have to living alongside each other, on and off the track, day after day. There will regularly be times when space is short, in a race and in the weighing-room, but harmony is pretty vital to our way of life. I'm not sure if it is so companionable on the flat but jump jockeys, with very few exceptions, get along pretty well.

Philip Hobbs was not coming racing, so I rang him from the weighing-room. It wasn't strictly necessary, as I know the horse so well, and luckily Philip seems to think enough of me now to let me use my own judgement in a race, accepting that there is little point in tying down a stable jockey with fussy instructions when so much can change. You might have two novice hurdles, for instance, each with 12 runners, and in one of them eight horses will want to make the running and in the other none at all. A good jockey must always be flexible; a good trainer will realise it.

Fontwell is an ideal course for the enigmatic Village King, because the figure-of-eight shape and constant undulations mean he has got something to think about all the way round. For a few strides, I thought he would spit the dummy out coming up the hill for the second time but he came back on the bridle once we turned away from the stands and raced with some decent enthusiasm. We jumped the last in front and my one moment of real anxiety came as he cocked his jaw and thought about stopping a few yards from the line. I managed to keep him going and to keep my balance and the only disappointing aspect of the winner was that the owners were not present to see it. The Heathcotes used to own Bula, who ran in rather better company than this old horse, but Village King was winning for the first time in a long while and it was rare for them to miss it.

Got away before the last race, beating some of the traffic queues back onto the A27, and had a good run home, albeit most of it after dark. Back home at 6.30pm, almost 13 hours after leaving. A bowl of pasta for supper and slob out in front of the TV for a couple of hours.

TUESDAY:

My knee aches. Nothing too bad, just a dull pain where a lot of weight work, aimed at strengthening the thigh muscle, has pulled the kneecap around a bit. I have no problem riding but if I'm hurrying around at home, or in a yard when riding out, it can get pretty sore. And I still limp, noticeably. People are telling me so and wondering out loud if the leg has healed properly. I know that it has and it really doesn't trouble me any more but the hobble is a mental thing - I got used to limping while I had no option and I now scarcely realise that I am favouring the other leg. I must start running during the summer, maybe play a few games of football, and get used to proper movement again. In the meantime, I can put up with a small ache and a conspicuous limp so long as I stay in one piece.

I did that alright today but I'm weary now. It's 9pm and I've just made it home from Sedgefield - that, after another early alarm call, this time at 6am. I was off to Henry Daly's yard, an hour's drive from my home. The bonus was that Mark Bradburne, who shares the stable rides with me, was heading in the same direction and came past to pick me up at 6.15. After yesterday, this was luxury - half-an-hour extra in bed and a chance to doze in the car.

Henry trains in the most idyllic spot imaginable, high above the ancient town of Ludlow at Downton Hall. He took over the licence from the late Capt. Tim Forster, his great mentor, and there is much about them that is similar. Like the Captain, Henry loved to train big, old-fashioned chasing types for owners who are predominantly of the old school themselves. He inherited a lot of them (horses and owners) from the Captain, of course, but they are loyal to him because he has the great Forster virtue of patience.

He also loved schooling, which is one of many reasons why we seem to get along so well. Once I am up there in his schooling ring, coaxing the young horses over the baby fences that are Henry's pride and joy, I am in my element. It helps, of course, if the day is as crisp and dry as it was this morning. No matter how hard I might try, the weather does affect my mood when riding out. No-one likes getting soaked and heavy rain during a schooling morning can put me in a dodgy frame of mind for the rest of the day - especially if I have forgotten to bring a change of clothes to wear going racing.

We schooled a dozen horses in a bit over an hour this morning, which was good going, but there was no time for breakfast. This was a shame, as I enjoy lingering at Downton Hall over tea and toast - it is a place of real character, a place I think I could live in myself, though I don't suppose I've any chance of evicting H.Daly.

Mark and I were on the road to Sedgefield before 9am. Mark drove, I slept. Perfect arrangement. Half way there, when Mark stopped for petrol, I forked out for a Kit-Kat to keep me going. We made it to the wilds of Co.Durham in time and I kept up the perfect start to the week. Like yesterday, it was one ride and one winner - good news for me but possibly even more so for Oliver Sherwood. A real high flier of the training ranks only a few seasons back, Oliver is living proof of the fickle nature of this game. His yard has been depleted both in quality and quantity and he has finally decided to uproot from Lambourn and set up shop elsewhere. Meantime, all winners are welcome, even if he has had to travel half the length of the country for this one.

Stayed long enough to witness one of the most bizarre races of the season - certainly one of the weirdest and most fortunate winners that Adrian Maguire will ever have against his name. The last fence had been dolled off, so there was a monumental run-in from the second last. Two horses duelled down the hill and one clearly interfered with the other a few yards from the line, causing the girl jockey of the second to fall off. The 'winner' was disqualified, the second had no rider so the race was awarded to Adrian, riding the third past the post. Some stroke of luck.

The jockey who had the race taken off him also got a hefty suspension - one of two ten-day bans handed out there today. There are times when you know you are in trouble and this was surely one of them. In my view, the standards of stewarding are more consistent than they were but there is still room for improvement. I suffered an injustice - at least in my eyes - at Stratford last summer when I got a little horse from the Hobbs yard up on the line to win what might have been his one and only victory, only to have the race taken off me for causing interference. Yes, there had been some but it was marginal and to my eye there was no way in which the stewards could say the result was affected. I felt extremely hard done-by and left feeling that stewards' panels still need an injection of fresh blood, preferably from ex-jockeys who know what it is to ride in a race, rather than on the hunting field, perhaps. I would be a supporter of full-time, professional stewards and of the public accountability that would come from the televising of inquiries.

All in all, there was a lot to talk about from the day's racing and I had a different driver to share it with. Mark was going on up to Scotland to do some schooling for his mother, who trains near Perth, so I begged a lift with Sam Stronge. He took me as far as Warwick and Zara drove out to pick me up. It's been a good day but I am ready for bed.

WEDNESDAY

More work, far less reward. After two days with a 100 per cent record it was down to earth with a thump today - five rides at Ludlow (generally one of my luckiest tracks) of which three were pulled-up and the best I could manage was a third. As if that was not sufficiently frustrating, the first four races here were all won by A.P., while the hurdler I could have ridden for Alan King at Doncaster, Chicago Bulls, won with complete authority. This sort of thing used to drive me mad but I'm much more philosophical now - I just rage silently. The fact is that I can't be in two places at one time but it is infuriating to have gone two days with only one ride on each and then find that I could have ridden four or five at each meeting today. In such circumstances, you are bound to get the choice wrong sometimes. It's nobody's fault, just maddening.

I rode out for Richard Phillips this morning, which meant a later departure time of 6.50. Richard can be a one-man comedy show when it suits him but he is far from being a joke as a trainer. After a brief spell at Jackdaws Castle, he is yet to move into another permanent base but is beginning to do okay in rented accommodation, ten minutes up the road from my house. Just rode the one lot, giving a spin to a horse called Another General, who is very progressive and has already won three on the bounce. I was on the road again at 8am and heading for the family home near Hereford to ride work on a couple for my mother. I help her out whenever I can and it was a simple diversion from the route to Ludlow.

Dreadful weather when I got to the track - raining in squalls amid very high winds. This certainly didn't help the horse I rode in the first, who has been 'tubed' to assist his breathing - it did him no favours with the gale whipping into it. It was cold enough for A.P.

to go out for one race with ear muffs on top of his riding cap. He got the message that he looked a fool and took them off for the next but, as he rode a winner in them, perhaps we should all be getting a pair.

Even with all the disappointments and the foul weather, it was still an important part of my job to speak to the owners after each race. We earn our living out of their horses but, for most of them at least, the sport is simply a hobby and I am a great believer that you should always try and find something constructive to say. That does not mean giving them so much flannel they go away with the idea that their useless beast is about to run up a sequence of wins. You have to be realistic and if I thought a horse was incapable of winning a race I would suggest as gently as I could that they might look elsewhere. Training fees are high and it makes more sense for an owner to sell and reinvest than plough on with something hopeless. Fortunately, even after five losers, I did not have to be so blunt today - all my rides could pick up a race in different conditions, though that was scant consolation as I made a rather bleak journey home in the fast-falling darkness. My nightly phone call to my mother was a touch monosyllabic. 'Shav' is staying tonight. I hope he's in the mood to cheer me up.

THURSDAY

Alan King wanted me for second lot, which suited fine. The trainer is getting thoughtful. His yard is pretty much on the way to Wincanton and it allowed me a lie-in until 7.15am - though I still had to de-ice the windscreen before setting off. A raw, wintry day and I was glad to drop the car at The Plough and hop in with Warren Marston, another mate from Jackdaws days.

In the build-up to Cheltenham, this is one of the most significant of midweek cards and probably Wincanton's biggest of the year. We're there early, which is just as well on several counts - we've beaten the traffic and I have plenty of time to get some physio on my back. It's been aching over the last few days, probably a reaction to getting back riding after a long absence, but it takes only a few minutes poking and prodding to put it right - I heard it click myself. 'Rabbit' Slattery is the woman with magic hands and we are always glad to see her. Until recently, it was a rarity to have a physiotherapist on hand during racing but more and more courses have now agreed to fund it. To my mind, it should be an automatic requirement of any raceday. You would not find any course neglecting to staff itself with gatemen and car park attendants, would you? Their jobs, essentially, are to keep public and vehicles moving smoothly and the physios do the same for jockeys. As we are part of the entertainment, or so I'm told, the small outlay required for this fundamental service should not be begrudged.

Moving more freely, I shower, shave and then do an interview for Channel 4. They are here covering today's racing but also getting plenty of material in the can for Cheltenham week. Jockeys do get a small fee (about £35) for TV interviews but I'm a fan of Channel 4 anyway - I think they do a really good job for racing.

Despite the usual hostile wind whipping across the hill, there is a decent crowd at Wincanton for a very competitive card. I have a good book of rides but I am not confident of a winner and I don't get one, instead hitting the bar with a second and a couple of thirds. It was good to see See More Business, a local hero in these parts, coming back to form in the Jim Ford Chase - good, too, for Joe Tizzard, who should now get to ride him in the Gold Cup. My main Cheltenham pointer from the day was a hurdler called Brother Joe, trained by Philip Hobbs and owned by Sir Robert Ogden. I thought the two-mile trip of the Kingwell Hurdle would be way too short for him but he ran really well to be third behind Hors La Loi III. Last time I rode him, I thought he had a few quirks but this was an honest performance and I left thinking he might have a realistic chance if upped in trip for the Stayers Hurdle.

I'd been back from injury for almost a month without a single fall but I had one today - in the paddock, of all things. It was a young horse of Richard Phillips's, quiet as a lamb at home but suddenly panicking in the claustrophobic atmosphere of a parade ring. I was decanted, bending my thumb back painfully as I hit the ground, but my good fortune was that the horse didn't tread on me - apparently it was close. He needed retacking, having broken his bridle in the fracas, but then behaved impeccably in the race and finished a promising third. It was a weird way to have my first fall of 2002 but reassuring to survive it relatively unscathed. There is no point in denying that it is in the back of my mind after a lay-off, just as the original injury is. Every now and again I have felt wary of the leg early in a race, though I haven't thought of it at all when I've been pushing and shoving at the business end.

The racecourse had a buzzy atmosphere today and I was just glad to be part of it after so long on the sidelines. The weighing-room, too, was an entertaining place to be. A.P. had a bad day - by his own standards, at least. No winners and a rodeo ride in the Jim Ford on Upgrade, who twice tried unsuccessfully to get rid of him. He'd actually performed miracles to stay on board but, naturally, got no credit for this from us. As for McCoy's lodger, Seamus Durack, he was in hilarious form all afternoon. Apparently, he's very intelligent but you'd never know it from some of the comments he comes out with.

Warren got us back to the Plough by 7 o'clock and it was only polite to stop for a drink. Home in good time for the supper Zara had cooked. She'd also taped the afternoon's racing and I reviewed it closely enough to know that I'm definitely not back riding how I want to be. There are several things I must work on - and Cheltenham is looming.

FRIDAY

Grim mood tonight. Cold, sore and deflated after a batch of rides at Warwick that included four favourites failed to produce a single winner. My thumb hurts, I'm shivering quivering with cold and frustration and all I want to do is go to bed and forget about it. These are the days as a jockey that I don't enjoy, the days when I start to question myself, the evenings when I become difficult to live with. This job is not all about fun and glory, far from it.

I was up at six this morning and on the road at a quarter past, making it to Henry Daly's place an hour later for another schooling session. Still bleary-eyed and longing for a drive, I chuckled on the way - almost the last laugh I was to have today - as I remembered the story of Rodney Farrant. 'Pigeon', as we call him, was doing well at the time, riding plenty of decent winners for Jenny Pitman in particular. One morning he was due to ride out for Henrietta Knight. Her yard, just outside Wantage, was close to Pigeon's home but he felt rough and decided to invent an excuse. He rang Henrietta and said he had two flat tyres - not one, just in case she suggested he put the spare on. Instead, Henrietta told him not to worry and that Terry (Biddlecombe, her husband) would drive round to pick him up. Defeated, the hapless Pigeon not only had to get up and dress in rapid time but also felt obliged to rush out to the road, where his car was parked, and let two of his own tyres down just to authenticate the story for Terry's eyes. It should stand as a lesson to us all. Every one of us struggles to get out of bed at times but you just have to get on with it. It wasn't long after that incident that 'Pigeon' gave up riding for a time and made the odd claim that Dave Roberts had ruined his career by mopping up all the spare rides for his team of jockeys. It was a short-sighted notion. Rodney had ridden plenty of winners but might have been forgetting the guiding principle of this racing life, which is that nothing comes to those who don't work for it.

One of his biggest successes was on Mudahim in the 1997 *Racing Post* Chase. This year's race is tomorrow and, as I've won the last two runnings, I've got more reason than most to look forward to it. After a day like today, it's nice to have something to hang onto.

Needed to see 'Rabbit' again this morning to get some strapping on my thumb. Plenty of time, despite stopping off at my accountants on the way from Ludlow to Warwick - I'm trying to put some money aside (at least in the months when I'm free from injury and earning some) and professional advice is welcome. My accountant also happens to be a big racing fan and it had not escaped his attention that I looked set for a good day. How this game can mock you, sometimes. Apart from blowing a gale again, it was spotting with rain when I got to Warwick. The ground was tacky and my confidence began to wane when my first ride, and first favourite, floundered. If he couldn't handle it, would the others? I soon found out. Normally, I enjoy riding round Warwick, relishing the challenge of the five fences down the back. Today, everything seemed to conspire against me. I even rode a favourite for Martin Pipe in a very weak race and trailed in third. Just to make matters worse, Zafarabad - a Philip Hobbs horse I could have ridden at Kempton but rejected on the grounds that I had far more fancied chances here - duly skated in. Straight home tonight, and not much chat over supper.

SATURDAY

What a difference. This week has taken me through the full range of emotions that this job has to offer. Monday and Tuesday I drove a long way for a single ride on each card, but both won. Perfect. For the next three days, I was far busier but failed to ride a single winner. Last night I felt weighed down by the cumulative effect of three days' disappointment, yet now I am on top of the world. I have won the *Racing Post* Chase for the third year running, I have ridden work on the horse that I feel could give me my second successive Cheltenham Gold Cup. Life is great. Fickle old world, isn't it?

Rode out in the snow this morning. Two strokes of luck, though - not enough snow to threaten racing and not far to drive - just down the road to Richard Phillips. To be honest, it was no penance, I was glad to be out and on horseback again to purge some of the frustrations of yesterday. I was back home, seeking hot drinks to warm me up, in time to watch 'The Morning Line', Channel 4's weekly racing magazine show. It's always lively, often argumentative. I'll listen to all their views, without necessarily agreeing with them.

In midweek, when I'm usually dashing straight from a morning's schooling, I will go racing in my riding-out kit and take something casual to change into later. Saturdays, along with all the big meetings like Cheltenham and Aintree, demand a suit. Properly dressed, it's my turn to drive to racing today, picking up 'Chocolate' and Tony Evans on the way. Kempton is an easy run at the weekends, the car park is great and the weighing-room one of the best around. As I have no rides until 3.30, there is even time for a game of pool. The valets win, as usual.

Gunther McBride is my big-race ride and, having won it on Gloria Victis and Young Spartacus, he has a lot to live up to in my eyes. He does the job brilliantly and this win was far more down to him than me. I don't know if this will be slated as a sub-standard *Racing Post* but my horse annihilated them, winning by 17 lengths. It's been a while since I have tasted a big winner and I had no intention of letting him idle, pushing him out right to the line. It feels great to ride such horses again, especially as there may be more to come from him later in the season.

After racing, I rode a strong piece of work on Looks Like Trouble and he felt fantastic. He'd been off a long time before winning impressively at Wincanton in January and Noel Chance is now taking him straight to Cheltenham. It's a sensible move and I can't wait for the day. Although I could have one or two options in the race - like Behrajan - I couldn't possibly desert him for this year's Gold Cup. If he stays sound, he will be a worthy favourite.

The mobile phone was working overtime on the way home. Warren and 'Shav' rang to say well done, which was good of them, and I got the expected call from David Nicholson. He may have retired but he has certainly not gone away and he was full of encouragement and good advice, as ever.

Back home, a quick change into dinner suit and off to the Eventers' Ball at Newbury. These do's are always good fun - especially on a Saturday night with something to celebrate - and I was reminded of the charity ball at Warwick one year, organised by Nick Skelton. Apart from being a top-flight showjumper, Nick had racehorses with 'The Duke' and we lads were asked to make up a table. The tickets included as much drink as you could hold and I have no doubt we abused the invitation. Probably, even in a gathering of 400, the Nicholson lads could be heard around the room. When it came to the auction, we were intent on bidding for something but some pretty lavish lots were selling for thousands, when fifty quid was about what we had in mind. Finally, our chance came - a pot-bellied pig was put up for auction and nobody wanted it. Gordon Clarkson, never slow in coming forward, bid 100 and suddenly we have a pig. "I'm sure the Duke will be delighted," the auctioneer said dryly.

The next morning, hungover and wondering what we had let ourselves in for, we were far from confident. Nervously, we told the guv'nor we'd bought something for the yard. To his credit, he didn't bawl us out and tell us to get rid of the thing, instead ordering us to build a pen by the sheds. We couldn't look after it properly, though, and after a couple of months Fred Hutsby said he would 'find a home for it'. I didn't enquire too closely what he meant by that.

Tonight, though, I keep my hands down during the auction. Usually, they were clutching a drink. It was a day to celebrate and I made a good job of it.

17.

Fifty-nine varieties

A jockey's view of Britain's racecourses

Judgements are always coloured by personal experience, and a jockey's view of a racecourse will be heavily influenced by how many winners he has had there, and how many falls. It's human nature. Until this year, I was ambivalent about Aintree - they could have banned the Grand National and I would not have shed a single tear. It just never gripped me the way Cheltenham does. I also had severe reservations about elements of the track and, yes, the National had not been kind to me - I'd never once got round and, three times, I had not even managed to survive as far as Canal Turn on the first circuit. After coming so close to victory on What's Up Boys in the 2002 National, I will now look at the race with more enthusiasm but I'm still not sure this will ever rank among my favourite venues.

It is not the National track - used only for four races each year - that worries me. The Mildmay course, which stages the huge majority of racing at Aintree, is just too sharp to be totally safe. It is not much bigger than Newton Abbot, which in turn is not much bigger than a dog track, yet it stages Grade One racing at inevitably high speeds. A lot of horses get injured there and I have to say I am not surprised. It is a very flat track and there is nothing to slow you down apart from the obstacles, which are consequently approached at a sometimes alarming speed. They say speed kills and it is as true on horseback as behind a wheel. Here, the fences come at you thick and fast - four of them down the back straight, which is probably one too many for the size of the circuit. The first fence in the back straight is notorious - it's upon you as soon as you come off the bend and a lot of horses simply struggle to put themselves right for it.

What we are talking about here is Grade One horses running round a Grade Two track, at high speed and frequently on fast ground. The pill is sugared at the April National meeting, partly by the atmosphere of anticipation but largely because the money is so good. Essentially, though, it is like running round Taunton for 100 grand. At Aintree's other meetings, the prize money is modest and the horses of considerably lower standard. I know of few jockeys who enjoy it, then.

The National course can be fantastic on a horse that jumps well. Winning the John Hughes Chase (now called the Topham Trophy again) on Gower-Slave was one of the headiest days of my career. If every ride round there was like that, I would love it. But you need a great deal of luck as well as a brave and agile horse and the combination is pretty rare. A lot of revisions have been made to the National course in the interests of safety and I think the Aintree management has done a fine job, both in this respect and by promoting and enhancing its big meeting. They can do nothing about the landscape of the Mildmay course, though, and that is its biggest problem. It is a sad fact that without the National itself, Aintree is the type of track that might struggle to survive.

Jockeys are not the most demanding of breeds. What they tend to expect of a course is that it should be as easy as possible to access and park the car and that the weighing-room should have functioning showers and sauna, sensible food and adequate space. Aintree just about manages this but, for a course of its stature, the weighing-room is ancient. There is plenty of room, though, and the only complaint about the decent sauna and the newly plumbed showers is that they are a long way apart. The car park is a bit of a trek, too, but we are lucky compared to the public, who have to park some way off-site, and face extensive security procedures, since the bomb scare of 1997. In a perverse way, that day remains a favourite memory of Aintree. Briefly, it was scary and certainly inconvenient - the National, after all, was about to be run when we were all summarily evacuated - but it turned into a night that none of us will ever forget. Everyone has their own story about the evening. Mine involved checking back into Liverpool's Adelphi Hotel, where they managed to find one room for what seemed like a dozen jockeys, and then going clubbing in the city in the only clothes we had - riding silks. I don't think I'll ever experience anything like that again. RATING: 6

ASCOT: Maybe I came along at the right time, so far as Ascot is concerned. I'm told the attitude there used to be haughty and the function of the staff seemed to be to keep everyone - jockeys included - out of the place. I've experienced none of that, which must mean that the modern management is doing a pretty good job. My experiences there have only been good and it is a course I look forward to riding at, not just for the track itself but because the facilities are so good. There is an excellent weighing-room, as you would expect of such a place, and the whole layout of our facilities is comfortable and established. The jockeys' food is prepared by a fellow called Matt, who has set up his own travelling business as what he calls 'Tea Boy to the Champions', and is much appreciated by all.

One gripe the jockeys have here is the confused signals from the course as to what our priorities should be between races. Ascot's authorities tend to want the winners to come out for a presentation ceremony with sponsors, which is understandable, but they then show annoyance if any jockey is late into the paddock - which is a long walk from the weighing-room. I hate being rushed around when I am riding. It makes everything feel awkward and I am prone to getting upset about it and losing my focus. Surely the solution is to have an extra five minutes between races to allow for the routines and the course layout?

All this may change when Ascot's radical redevelopment is complete, as there is talk of moving the paddock. The other talk about the place recently has been that jump racing may be dropped due to a shortage of runners in valuable sponsored races. While I can understand the concern, I think people may be looking at this the wrong way. It is true that Ascot frequently has single-figure fields racing for a lot of money but generally the standard of horse is high. Surely it is better to have a six-runner race of evident quality, in which any of the six could win, than have 16 runners of which only two have any genuine chance, as happens often elsewhere.

I believe it would be a crying shame if Ascot did away with jumping. We simply can't afford to lose a course of this quality. It is a very good track to ride round, so big that you never need to be in a hurry. From Swinley Bottom, a distant point from the stands, there are still four hurdles to jump and it's all uphill, deceptively so in the straight itself.

In a sense, it is much easier to ride courses like this and it is on the smaller, tighter tracks, where things happen so quickly and position is so vital, that a spectator can get a better idea of how good a jockey is. At Ascot, as at Newbury, Wetherby and the like, the best horse will win, nine times out of ten. The steeplechase fences are big and testing and it is not a place to take a modest novice chaser for experience, but that is quite right in my book. Ascot has a reputation to uphold, and if that means it puts on valuable races for small but elite fields, I feel it is doing its job as a top-of-the-range track. RATING: 8

AYR: The first time I went to Ayr, I thought the place was stuck in a 1920s time-warp. Its weighing-room was in a bowels of an ancient, flaky grandstand and the facilities were a disgrace. Since then, they have built a modern, stand-alone jockeys' block, which is smart, fully functional and a decent example for others to follow. I'm told some of the facilities for the public still languish in another age but jockeys can now have no complaints about the place. Around Scotland, indeed, there is a sense of purpose and progress about the racecourses that make them a pleasure to visit, on the relatively rare occasions when I get the chance.

For we southern jockeys, the annual opportunity to ride at Ayr comes in late April at the Scottish Grand National meeting. It's over two days now, a Friday and a Saturday, and most jockeys - and a good few trainers - would be delighted if it was restored to three. It comes at a time of the season when most of us are happy to relax. Cheltenham and Aintree are past, the Sandown finale meeting is all that remains, so Ayr is a fun festival which all of us enjoy to the full. Most of the crowd stay in one hotel, the Caledonian in mid-town, so the atmosphere is convivial and big groups of us will go out together. The night-life on a Friday evening in Ayr is good and, up to a point (there is a prestigious four-mile chase to ride the following day, after all) we will take advantage of it. I remember during my early riding days with David Nicholson, bumping into 'The Duke' in a bar after 10.30pm on the Friday night. As I was riding for him in the Scottish National the following day, I was scared he might explode, but not a bit of it - he was well into the swing.

Being on the west coast, a long way even from the M6/M74 motorway, it is a pretty remote course for southern-based riders to reach by road and the experience is a whole lot more comfortable by air. Unlike the Flat jockeys, who we considered outrageously pampered in such matters, we hardly ever fly to meetings but I try to make an exception for Ayr. This last year, a chartered light aircraft took half-a-dozen of us up and, with the costs divided, it was not too punishing on the pocket and a great deal less stressful than sitting in the car for five hours each way. Having a few winners added to the enjoyment and, as ever, I am prejudiced in favour of Ayr because I've tended to be lucky there. Most jockeys would agree, though, that is a fair, galloping track, with good fences, though when the ground is on the fast side - as it often is in April - you do need to be on a horse with natural speed in order to lay up with the pace. RATING: 7

BANGOR: Without wishing to insult the locals, I think Bangor is a place you would be most unlikely to visit if it was not for the racecourse - even assuming you knew which Bangor staged racing, which cannot be taken for granted. There is another Bangor on the tip of north-west Wales and a third Bangor, a ferry port, in northern Ireland. Strange though it may sound, racing legend is littered with tales of trainers dispatching horseboxes to both these towns by mistake. The correct Bangor is a tiny, nondescript village off a winding road between Wrexham and Whitchurch - a blink-and-you-miss-it place of a few houses, a couple of riverside pubs and a shop. It's pleasant enough but hardly memorable. The course is just outside the village and it is easy to believe you are on the wrong road until you suddenly come upon the entrance. Part of the reason for its anonymity is that it has no grandstand - the only such course in the country. It relies on its natural grass banks to provide vantage points for the spectators, which is fine on a sunny day but not so clever in the rain.

Despite all this, Bangor has a jolly atmosphere, with a good, local crowd guaranteed, and I quite enjoy it as I've been top jockey there for a couple of years. My main supplier of suitable rides is Henry Daly, whose Ludlow yard almost makes him a Bangor local. Henry's speciality is big, old-fashioned chasers who are tailor-made for the long-distance races on heavy ground that are so easily associated with Bangor.

There seems to be no happy medium here - the ground is either very fast or very soft. Being next to a river, it can be barely raceable at times during wet winters and spectators have to put up with parking in a waterlogged field. The jockeys' car park is also a field - thankfully, not quite such wellington-boot territory - but the weighing-room is a recent, purpose-built block with perfectly adequate facilities. Considering this is a small course, with little money to flash around, and that it suffered severely during the foot-and-mouth epidemic as well as its annual battle with waterlogging, I am just pleased to see it still operating and, at its own level, thriving. It would be easy to think that a course with so little going for it must be vulnerable to closure but I am in the camp that believe the diversity of courses is a great strength of British racing and that all of them should be preserved if possible. RATING: 5

CARLISLE: This is one of the best tracks in the country for proper National Hunt horses - those that are bred to jump. I first rode there for Lucinda Russell, who was my earliest training contact in the north, but these days I encourage all the trainers I ride for regularly to go up there, especially with horses having a first run over fences. Henry Daly is now doing it regularly, despite a black day last year when he sent up four suitable candidates, three of which I thought could win. We came home empty-handed after two fallers and two also-rans but thankfully it hasn't deterred Henry.

The track is a northern version of Towcester, with its undulations and its stiff uphill finish. Like Towcester, it also produces some searchingly soft ground - this is a part of the country that seems to get an awful lot of rain. It is ideal for old-fashioned horses that set out simply to gallop and jump and, for a jockey, it is a place where there is no need to get into a rush. Going away from the stands, the ground falls away fast but the fences are well positioned and I have never thought any of them are dangerous. The home straight is long and relentlessly uphill, which means you can be four or five lengths down at the third-last and still feeling comfortable, so long as your horse is travelling well. You can ride a waiting race here far more effectively than on sharp tracks such as Taunton. Consequently, it is also a good place to educate horses and it is significant that top trainers such as Lenny Lungo like to send the pick of their stable here.

For the past year or so, the downside of a day at Carlisle has been that the place is a building site. The old main stand has been demolished and it has been as much as the course can do to provide the most basic spectator facilities while the construction work goes on. Some of the public may feel they would have been better advised to close for a year but I admire them for continuing. I just hope that the new stand includes an adequate weighing-room to replace the tiny, damp and primitive building that is still in use now, its only redeeming feature being the cheery tea-lady who provides our food. RATING: 6

CARTMEL: The first-timer at Cartmel, walking the course to familiarise himself for his rides, will be understandably worried when he comes into the home straight. The track is on top of the village at this point and a stone wall runs along its perimeter, with mattresses tied to the wall to cushion the impact for anyone unlucky enough to be thrown in that direction by a freak fall. It is a crude safety measure but, in fairness, there are no obstacles to be jumped alongside the wall. In fact, there is nothing to jump at all for the final half-mile on the steeplechase course, which makes this the longest run-in in the country - quite something for a track that is barely one mile round.

It's a one-off place, Cartmel, and simply cannot be compared with any other course. The Cumbrian village is tiny and atmospheric, with a market square surrounded by pubs, and each raceday just takes the place over. It's one massive fairground, really, and once you have got over the initial shock it is a whole lot of fun. When I first went, I couldn't understand why their three-day Bank Holiday meetings would be staged on a Saturday, Monday and Wednesday. Finally, it was explained to me that they need a spare day just to clear up the mountain of litter left by crowds which can get up to 25,000 if the sun shines at the end of August. What some bigger, smarter courses would give for crowds like that. It does create some horrific traffic problems but the course and local police have done their best to alleviate the worst of the congestion by devising one-way systems through the surrounding country lanes. Nevertheless, if I'm riding in the last, I will tend to linger and have a drink in one of the marquees rather than plunge straight into the home-going hordes.

The facilities here, all of them in centre-course, are spartan. There is one small stand, which has no roof in order that spectators can see all round the circuit. The weighing-room, at ground level, is small and cramped and there is no sauna - I've tended to have a run round the track before racing when the weather is warm. In time, as the new funding streams work their way through the system, I hope Cartmel will receive sufficient money to improve the facilities without sacrificing any of the special atmosphere - a tricky balance to strike - but the racedays here are so rare and so different from anything else that it would be a churlish jockey who complained too much.

There are rural rituals here that you don't find anywhere else. Every jockey who rides a Cartmel winner is presented with a sticky toffee pudding, for which the village shop has now become nationally known. I've never developed a taste for it and, one year, I was there for the whole three-day meeting and got four puddings, which sat in my cupboard at home for ages. If I ride a Cartmel winner now, I give the pudding to the grateful northern valets.

There is no point in bringing Carlisle or Towcester horses to Cartmel. A nimble, quick animal is what is required here. On the right type, the course is not bad, despite its sharpness, though I wonder what went on in the section that disappears into the woods before the days of patrol cameras - I imagine a few younger jockeys were put in their place by the elder statesmen. Strange things do still happen here. A few years back, I rode a horse called Name of

Our Father for Peter Bowen and, with the race at our mercy, the weight cloth started to slip off halfway up the run-in. Disqualification is automatic if you return without such equipment but I managed to grab it as it fell and passed the post with the reins in one hand and the weightcloth in the other. Only at Cartmel... RATING: 4

CATTERICK: This is the one jumping course in the country where I have yet to ride a winner and, consequently, I don't like it. In truth, it would not be a favourite even if I had got on the scoreboard there long ago, for it is a fundamentally bleak and unappealing spot with a standard of racing to match. I have probably not ridden there more than half-a-dozen times and I am keen to go back only in order to complete my set of winners. My memories of it are unflattering - low-grade, start-of-the-week racing under leaden skies with virtually nobody watching. Was it really that bad?

Of course, tracks like this are essential to meet the market for racing on Mondays and Tuesdays, both as a betting medium and for those trainers whose horses are unlikely to win anywhere more competitive. Some places, though, do it far better than others and although Catterick has made an effort to upgrade its facilities, spending money on the weighing-room and installing a sauna quite recently, the atmosphere remains sterile.

The track itself suffers from overuse. This is a dual-purpose course, Flat and jumping, and it stages meetings 12 months of each year. The grass therefore gets little chance to grow back and some areas of the track are actually more brown than green. The bends, in particular, have been a mess on certain occasions I've ridden there and the fact that they are rough and ungrassed is a significant deterrent to anyone thinking of sending a decent horse there. I appreciate that it is a dilemma for such courses, who probably need regular meetings in order to balance the books, but standards will never improve if ground conditions are not widely trusted. RATING: 3

CHELTENHAM: The Festival is the best three days of the year, beyond question, but even on quieter days, when the crowds are small and the stakes not so high, Cheltenham is definitely the best place in the country to ride a winner. Whether it is the history of the course or the theatrical layout, there is something about the atmosphere that is inspiring to a jockey, no matter how many times he might have been round there.

As a child, I had been taken along by my parents, but the first working day I had there was in 1994, when I led up a horse for David Nicholson in the Supreme Novices Hurdle. It was an eye-opening experience for a 16-year-old to be in front of such crowds. Later, I was back in the stable yard when Flakey Dove was brought in after winning the Champion Hurdle. His lad turned out to be someone who had worked on our family farm for a year. It suddenly seemed quite a small world again.

Jockeys can have no gripes about their facilities here and even the weighing-room food - served by a friendly woman called Sandy who has been there as long as I can recall - is way above the average. If you want something they haven't got, they will generally go and find it. The jockeys are made to feel appreciated, which is not always the case elsewhere.

The track itself has many good memories for me, notably the Gold Cup on Looks Like Trouble and the Champion Chase on Flagship Uberalles, but inevitably there have been some brutal disappointments, none worse than in 1996. Just two years after leading up at the Festival for the first time, I found myself riding the short-priced favourite for the Sun Alliance Chase. Mr Mulligan was much the best horse I had ridden at that time and, having already won the Reynoldstown Chase on him at Ascot, I'd naively convinced myself that he must win at Cheltenham. Nothing, though, went to the planned script - we were slowly away, he made a mistake at the first fence and I was always chasing the pace after that. We did get to the front, only to be caught on the final climb by Nathen Lad. As a teenager I should perhaps have been delighted to finish second in a championship race but it felt like the end of the world.

Looking back, that race was an example of what can happen at the Festival, where in my view the best horses do not always win. Only at Cheltenham in March are races run at such a helter-skelter speed and it can sometimes be counter-productive, bringing some odd results and leaving a mark on horses from which some struggle to recover.

Experience of the undulations brings its own wisdom. You do need a horse with gears to hold a position in the Festival races but if you are still going well jumping the last uphill fence, it is a tremendous feeling, because you can make up your ground on the long sweep down towards the home straight and have something in hand for the hill. My dislike about Cheltenham is confined to the times when I ride a horse that is essentially not good enough to be there. At Newbury or Chepstow, where the pace tends to be steadier and the terrain is not so demanding, even an inadequate horse can comfortably stay in touch for two-thirds of a race. At Cheltenham, the speed of the races accounts for casualties, especially at the downhill fences, where you are desperate to meet them on the right stride but only the better horses can do it. Approaching those fences on a fundamentally incompetent jumper is one of the worst feelings I've known as a jockey. RATING: 9

CHEPSTOW: I have a few pet hates about Chepstow, the first of which is that I resent having to pay to get into Wales. Once there, I've encountered a few gatemen too fond of the authority that their badge endows. Then, having endured the changeover period in a portacabin while the recent building work at the course was completed, it was infuriating to turn up for the grand opening of the new weighing-room and find that it did not even meet the basic requirement of sufficient space. It is beyond me why courses do not consult jockeys and valets when they are rebuilding - I honestly don't think we are difficult to please and wasting a new structure simply by making it too small is shambolic.

They knocked the old weighing-room down, though probably only just before it fell down of its own accord. It was a primitive structure that seemed to be permanently freezing cold. The showers seldom worked properly and the sauna was tiny. I was pleased to vacate it, encouraged that Sir Stanley Clarke's Northern Racing company had taken over and appeared to be getting things moving. Despite the inadequacies of the new weighing-room, I have little doubt that Chepstow will continue to advance, given the level of investment, because the catchment area is good and the course itself is acknowledged as one of the best in the country on which to educate a horse.

Because it has an exceptionally long straight, with five fences and four hurdles. a jockey can hold onto his horse all the way down the back and for some way afterwards. Watching a race here, it is common to see lots of horses still travelling well turning for home but very few left in contention by the second-last obstacle.

I like riding round here and it is a place where fortune has smiled on me. On Easter Monday, last season, I drove across the bridge thinking I was pretty unlikely to ride a winner but I came home with four, including two for the local trainer Paul Rich, who only has three horses in his yard. I've had few days so good and Paul had certainly had none.

The one serious pitfall on the course comes just past the winning post, where the track falls away rapidly downhill before turning sharply left-handed for a short but steep climb. The stable exit is at the foot of the hill and horses are aware of it, so some are reluctant to make the turn. The problem is accentuated by a woodchip road crossing on which a horse I was riding a few years back stumbled and came down - I broke my collarbone in the fall. It is not so much a design fault as a product of the geography but it is a tricky area to negotiate, especially on a horse that is fresh and pulling hard. All you do know is that if you steer him safely round the turn, he won't be pulling by the time he reaches the top of the hill. RATING: 7

DONCASTER: This is one of those courses that seem to think the ideal snack for a jockey between rides is a stodgy pasty. For all our subtle hints that something lighter might be better, they are not easily dissuaded, so I have to conclude that catering is not a strong point. The tea room is very small but at least they have pandered to our needs by putting in a fridge loaded with soft drinks. I tend to have half a glass of coke for refreshment but some will drink cans of Red Bull for its energy value. It's all down to personal preference but I try and avoid such drinks during racing, on the basis that if you have it all the time your body begins to crave it.

The weighing-room here is elegant, elaborate and very old. There is no chance of them knocking it down and starting again - visually it is the nicest feature of the course - but it is certainly in need of some interior refurbishment. Doncaster itself is now a sprawling industrial town that seems to spread further each time I go there. No obvious signs of any recession here and, on the face of it, the busy, dual-purpose track should be flourishing. It certainly attracts some decent horses but while it stages the highest class of Flat racing it is seen by most jumps trainers as a good stepping stone to something better.

The track drains almost too well for its own good, so the ground is often quick. The fences are stiff, penalising all but the best jumpers, and there is a potential trouble spot after the winning post, with a bend that is just too sharp for National Hunt horses. Setting off in a two-mile hurdle race, especially on juveniles that are keen and green, it can be quite an undertaking to get them around this first turn.

Thereafter, the track is broad and suits galloping types but, far too often, jockeys get racing in earnest too early here. Coming off Rose Hill, the farthest point from the stands, you can see them jostling for positions as if there is only a two-furlong straight to come.. In fact it is more than half-a-mile to the post after turning in and there is plenty of time to make a telling move. RATING 6

EXETER: This is the best track in Britain for a novice chaser. The reason is simple - apart from two fences which are jumped on level ground, the rest are all uphill. To those who have never ridden, this may seem a perverse recommendation but a horse's rhythm and confidence is far more at risk when jumping downhill, with the ground falling away, than up. I have known horses win at Exeter when they are virtually incapable of winning anywhere else.

Karratha, who won a number of hurdle races for Philip Hobbs, was neither a brave horse nor particularly impressive at his obstacles and he jumped poorly over fences at a number of tracks - the exception was Exeter, where he recorded his only win.

This is far from being a haven for inadequates, though. Top trainers love it as a place to bring their most exciting young novices, doubtless to the frustration of the West Country yards that are struggling to pick up a prize at their local track. Most of my winners there have been for the Hobbs yard and it was also here, on a Hobbs horse, that I suffered my worst injury. Ilico, who had won over hurdles at Aintree late the previous season, was the perfect example of a highly promising novice chaser being taken to Exeter for experience. Sadly, it was as far as he was to get and the fall that caused his death also broke my leg. It was no fault of the course, nor even of the horse, who had come from France and been schooled intensively from the age of two - it was just one of those incidents that can happen in any race, especially amongst novices, in which one horse is blinded by another as he approaches a fence. It was a bad blow for me but, equally, a severe setback for Philip's stable, where they had been banking on Ilico to develop into a leading novice.

The fall was lodged unhelpfully in my mind the next time I came to jump that fence, some four months later. When I was younger and new to the game, I could never remember a particular fence on any course. Now, maybe through being more relaxed in my riding, I seem to have more time to think during a race. In this instance, I wished for memory blackout. As it turned out, I negotiated the obstacle perfectly well, though oddly enough I had taken another fall earlier in the day - this time over hurdles - during my first ride back at the track. The ambulance man, twisting the knife a little, said: 'You're not having much luck round here, are you?'

Actually, though, he is mistaken. I've had a lot of luck at Exeter and I look forward to every visit - except, perhaps, at those times of year when the Devon holiday traffic turns the M5 into an elongated car park. On normal days, it is an easy journey for me and the course is hard by the main A38 dual carriageway. The weighing-room is spacious, comfortable and neatly close to the paddock and there is a relatively new sauna. Only the food lets the place down - it's pre-prepared sandwiches left on a plate to shrivel. RATING: 7

FAKENHAM: Set in a charming corner of Norfolk, Fakenham is run by a lovely bunch of people and the prize money is surprisingly good. Why, then, does the very thought of having to go there fill me with such dread that if I never had to ride there again I would regard it as something to celebrate?

Well, the journey has a fair bit to do with it. North Norfolk might be a smashing spot to spend a weekend but for a jockey plying his trade it is inconvenient to say the least. Get to Huntingdon and it feels as if you are nearly there - in fact there is still two hours ahead on single-carriageway roads where overtaking is almost as difficult as riding a waiting race on the track that awaits. Fakenham is barely a mile round and could hardly present a greater contrast to somewhere like Exeter. You jump a fence, turn a bend, jump another fence, turn another bend and so on, until you almost feel an attack of dizziness coming on. Horses win here that can win nowhere else and, for some reason, it is not always the small and nippy types - Pam Sly trains a horse called Bassenhally who is essentially slow, yet the turns of Fakenham seem to light him up.

There has been some rebuilding here in recent times but the ancient structure that houses the weighing-room is surely ready to be condemned. The jockeys' quarters are tiny and, during the winter, often cold and damp. There is no sauna, a very rare omission on modern racecourses, and even the showers do not always work efficiently, so I have occasionally been decanted into the rush-hour traffic for the pleasures of a four-hour drive home feeling grubby and unwashed. Other courses have shown that a basic but modern weighing-room - essentially, no more than a small bungalow - need not cost the earth and I hope Fakenham heed the example. Meantime, no offence to those who are trying their best to promote the place but I shall hope I'm sent elsewhere whenever they have a raceday. RATING: 2

FOLKESTONE: Rumours have abounded that Folkestone may soon be shut down as a racecourse, with the land being sold off to developers. It must speak volumes that, with the exception of a handful of local trainers, very few would mourn its passing. Like Fakenham, its standing with racing professionals suffers through its location as much as its poor facilities - tackling the M25 and M20 is a deterrent in itself and I would not personally care if they cut it off and let it float across the Channel so that the French could race round it. Its jump racing is staged mostly on Mondays, with poor horses taking part and a lack of crowds and atmosphere. It is one of those venues that serve a purpose chiefly by putting on racing for the betting shops - though why anyone should wish to bet on most of the fare down here is beyond me. Look through an a average Folkestone card and it is common to find three awful races - sellers, claimers and the lowest grade of handicaps - with a scarcity of recent winners, alongside three novice races in which there might be the odd promising horse. Hence, half the races might have an odds-on favourite required to do little more than gallop round and the other half are painful to watch.

I had a bad experience there last year, when a horse trained by my mother broke a leg. Although it is pretty sharp, the track itself is not too bad apart from an area just past the stands, where for some reason the ground seems to deteriorate into a series of ridges that have seen a number of horses stumble dangerously.

Folkestone salvages some marks by its facilities for jockeys, which are not lavish but can generate little criticism. The weighing-room is of a standard design that seems to be used by other south-east courses like Fontwell and Plumpton. Changing areas are roomy, the sauna and showers are functional and there is a decent tea room. It is a simple template for small courses to follow and, for that, the place must be commended. RATING: 2

FONTWELL PARK: Since Windsor closed its gates to jump racing, Fontwell has become the only figure-of-eight steeplechase track around. It makes it an interesting course to ride, though not always an enjoyable one. The downhill fences, cutting through the middle of the 8, have a tricky drop on the landing side and some of the moderate horses that race round here tend to knuckle over. It is a fast track and, thankfully, the groundstaff make fences of a sensible size and texture, so that the horses can brush through the top of them. Sandown-type fences here would be inviting accidents.

Unsurprisingly, the shape of the track encourages course specialists and there are some canny older horses who seem to flourish for coming here. Philip Hobbs brought Village King here last season and, considering he has earned the dreaded Timeform squiggle as being unreliable, he really enjoyed himself, the twists and turns giving him something to think about throughout the race. The same applies to jockeys, of course, because on a figure-of-eight it is impossible to ride a race around the inner - you are there for one bend, then on the outside for the next. You have to be particularly alert about positioning round here.

The hurdles track, being a more orthodox oval, is comparatively straightforward but the race will usually develop in earnest on the downhill back straight and there can be some unpleasant falls at the third-last hurdle with horses just being asked to go quicker than they are capable. Although I never like refusing rides, I will be careful at Fontwell and Dave Roberts, my agent, is very protective - basically, if the form of an offered spare is poor, or his jumping suspect, the risk is not sustainable.

Fontwell trades on many a winter Monday, just like Folkestone, but it is far more popular course. It is well-managed, with steadily enhanced facilities, and cleverly promoted and the reward is some very decent crowds, especially during the summer. Part of the drive here has been to attract good sponsors for prestige races, which is an admirable aim, but I wonder whether a valuable hurdle race with only four or five runners does the course much more good than its run-of-the-mill handicaps with 15. Possibly, a thriving track like this should be looking to increase its minimum prize money - hopefully to around 5,000 - rather than putting so much of the pot into a few races.

No complaints about the facilities here - but one particularly amusing memory. A couple of years back, my friend and great rival, A.P.McCoy, was waving his stick so vigorously to get his horse up the final hill that he unbalanced himself and fell off, 20 yards from the line. He was thankfully quite unharmed but it was such a stunningly rare sight that the rest of us quite enjoyed it. We get so few reasons to believe that he might have human fallabilities after all. RATING:3

HAYDOCK PARK: With generous prize money on offer, a lovely galloping track and generally good horses to ride round it, I can't help but like Haydock - it ranks in the elite few, so far as I am concerned, and I can find very little to criticise about it. I am conscious of being lucky, though, in the quality of my rides and I can understand that a jockey who averages only a dozen or so winners each year might have a more jaundiced view of a track where the racing is so highly competitive. There is nothing worse than going to a meeting with the near-certain knowledge that your only ride is going to be trailing around at the back of the field.

Haydock sponsored me for a year, which doubtless helps me think well of the place, but that experience allowed me to see at close quarters how a top racecourse should be run. It's a proper business, the buildings in use for many non-racing activities, and the revenue raised has enabled them to steadily upgrade the raceday facilities, so that it is now one of the smartest and· most· modern of courses, with a real 21st century feel. A new weighing-room is among the recent additions and, unlike certain other courses, they got it absolutely right in terms of space and amenities, which are first-class.

Situated within sight of the M6 motorway, it is one of the best-placed courses, easily accessed even by southern jockeys and trainers, and my only complaint would be that ten days of jump racing here does not seem enough. There was a time when the fences were too intimidating and the field sizes for the valuable chases here were consequently small. It was a lesson that there is simply no point in building fences too big. Some trainers will be discouraged from running at all, while spectators can quickly lose interest in a steeplechase in which four set out and only two get round. You still need a horse with scope to jump round Haydock but the fields are better now and the product has improved all round. It's a top spot - I would just like to go there more often.

RATING: 9

HEREFORD: As a boy, Hereford was very much my local track, so it is only natural that I have an enduring affection for it. It is not as pretty a place as the area merits - the view from the stands is of car dealerships and housing estates - but for me the memories are more important than the scenery. I rode my first winner there, in a hunter chase on my grandfather's Rusty Bridge, and most of my early rides were round Hereford. Old Rusty seemed to run at almost every meeting, while Richard Lee and Milton Bradley, two of the trainers who gave me a teenage opportunity, ran a lot of horses here. For me, it was as much a gathering of family and friends as a place of work. To some extent, the same still applies today. Each May, the course stages the Ivor Johnson Memorial Hunter Chase, a fitting tribute to grandad. My father comes to a lot of the meetings and I tend to take the chance to drop in at home, either before or after racing.

My sense of belonging is sometimes lost on the gatemen, who have been especially officious over the years but seem to be improving now that the track has come under the Stan Clarke banner. I shall be fascinated to see the direction and level of new in investment here. There is no doubt the public facilities need upgrading, though the crowd here tends to be dominated by local folk, many of them farmers, and they are probably not as demanding as some.

It is a straightforward track to ride, a 12-furlong circuit shaped like a square, and although the jockeys' amenities are anything but lavish, the weighing-room has been slightly modernised and a sauna belatedly installed. It will never be plush but, for me, that hardly matters. RATING: 7

HEXHAM: They race four times in June at Hexham these days and it is then that I am most likely to be found there. It is an eight-hour round trip for me to this ancient Northumberland outpost but I don't begrudge it, especially if I can link it up by riding at Cartmel or Perth either side of the meeting. Hexham is a lovely if isolated spot which draws a happy local crowd - if the weather is fine, the atmosphere is so good that even jockeys notice it. Unlike some, I really enjoy the summer programme of jumping and I find it much easier to ride at the rural courses when the sun is shining.

They plainly struggle for money at Hexham and were hit harder than most courses by the foot-and-mouth restrictions in 2001. It's the sort of track that is constantly vulnerable, in a commercial sense, and if racing did ever stop here it is hard to see it being restored. With that in mind, it is worth saying that the groundstaff do an outstanding job and invariably produce a good racing surface. The back straight runs downhill but the fences are well-made and seem to cause few problems. The weighing-room is what you would expect of a country track - nothing extravagant but essentially big enough to cope. RATING: 3

HUNTINGDON: As jump courses go, this must be the flattest, and just about the fastest in the country. You need a horse with speed to lay up round here, though the lack of any gradients means that jockeys sometimes start racing in earnest much too far out. You will frequently see the leaders being pushed along vigorously three from home, which means the slower types sometimes have a chance to get back into a race.

It is a good track for introducing speedy hurdlers to fences, because there are so few complications, no reason for them to do anything stupid. Old-fashioned chasing types might struggle, though. I rode Behrajan here as a novice and although he did win he was always labouring to maintain the pace and consequently made more mistakes than he ever did at courses like Newbury. It is a simple fact that a horse has a cruising speed and Behrajan was being asked to exceed his.

They draw consistently good crowds here and one of the features is the open ditch in front of the stands. Spectators love seeing horses tested right in front of them and I have no quarrel with that so long as the fence rides well, which in this case it does.

Facilities for jockeys are basic but acceptable and my main worry concerns the winners' enclosure which fronts it - it is so cramped that there is a constant risk of a horse, either irritable or panicky, kicking out and causing injury. I appreciate there is a premium on space but I do think it is something that should be looked at. Jockeys in general also miss the benign presence of Hugo Bevan, a great character who was clerk of the course here for many more years than most of our careers will last. Hugo, who was at school with my father, was always very honest with us about the state of the ground, even if he had problems. Everyone respected that and it has to be the sensible way for all courses to act - why waste time on lies that will quickly be exposed? RATING: 6

KELSO:There is a particular feature to a winter's afternoon in the old weighing-room at Kelso - an open coal fire to gather round for warmth. Sedgefield used to have one, too, but since they built a new weighing-room this is the only one of its kind, and it is a welcome bonus on some of the afternoons I have experienced up there. They do, incidentally, have a sauna, too, for more authentic sweating.

It is on my pretty rare visits to courses like Kelso that I appreciate the friendliness of the northern jockeys. It would be easy for them to resent people like me going into their territory and, by extension, pinching their rides, but they are unfailingly welcoming. I only hope they think the same about us when they come south.

Kelso's position, remote from any major city, makes it an especially difficult journey - it is fully an hour from the nearest airport so there is no real alternative to the five-hour drive for me. Recently, I undertook it for one ride in a novice hurdle and, when it was duly beaten, I spent the five-hour return journey wondering why on earth I had bothered. Any horses that make the journey from the south must inevitable travel the previous day and it is a fact that long journeys and nights away suit some horses no better than some humans - they just won't run their race afterwards.

Once there, this is a nice track, especially over fences. The chase course suits galloping types and attracts plenty of decent ones in the valuable staying handicaps they run here now. My first winner there, for John Wade, was in the Durham National, which had been switched from Sedgefield due to bad weather, but Kelso is now a preferred venue for top northern trainers and Ferdy Murphy, for instance, has run Paris Pike there more than once. The hurdles course is much sharper - only a little more than a mile round - and reminds me of a left-handed Taunton. RATING: 3

KEMPTON PARK: Other than the nearby M25, which casts an unwelcome shadow over the place on Friday evenings, Kempton has a great deal going for it - easy to access, great weighing-room, nice track. Why, then, did I dislike it so much for the first few years of my career? Easy - I struggled to ride a winner there. Fortune has turned around completely now. After a near miss on King Lucifer (I think I should have won), I have won the last three runnings of the February feature race, the *Racing Post* Chase. First it was the ill-fated Gloria Victis (a spare ride when A.P. was suspended), then Young Spartacus and finally Gunther McBride. Unsurprisingly, I love Kempton now.

Familiarity round here is a great help. Kempton's jumps track is an unusual, triangle shape and, because it is very flat, there is really nowhere to give a horse a breather. You cannot let the leaders get away from you down the back straight - the second leg of the triangle - because they will seldom come back, so tactical awareness is all-important. Horses need to travel well through a race, to be quick on their feet and intelligent enough to know what they are doing. Good, quick jumping is priceless here.

Being a suburban London track, Kempton can feel dour on the quiet days. Go there on a midwinter Wednesday and it seems there is no-one around at all but, by contrast, Saturdays are invariably buzzy and the big meetings, especially at Christmas, have a rousing atmosphere. The public facilities have been extensively modernised of late and another change has seen the paddock and winners enclosure moved directly behind the main stand, which definitely adds to the sense of spectacle and theatre.

The winning jockey has to weigh-in in public, in a booth next to the paddock, but if innovations like this give spectators a clearer insight into the whole racing experience I am all for them. So long as they don't open up the weighing-room to inspection - especially this one, which has the novelty factor of a pool table on which we jockeys are consistently beaten by the valets. RATING: 8

LEICESTER: Think of Leicester and I think of maiden chases. They love them here - usually about 18 in the field, many of them suspect jumpers. If you are without a ride, you often feel quite pleased. On a good jumper, this is a nice enough course to ride round but in a field of 18 maidens over fences there is a good chance that a dozen will be useless and there are plenty of potential pitfalls for them here.

The back stretch runs downhill, quite sharply at one point. Three-mile chases start at the top of the back straight, the first three obstacles are all jumped downhill and the fences come thick and fast. An inexperienced chaser can jump one of these obstacles well enough and stumble on the landing side, bringing down others who are trying to get their balance. I've seen three or four in a heap at the end of the back straight and it is here that the course is at its narrowest, which creates additional hazards. None of this discourages leading trainers from coming - it was always a favourite course of David Nicholson's and Henry Daly and Nicky Henderson are invariably represented these days.

Another idiosyncrasy of Leicester is its ground. As often as not, it will be perfect good ground over fences but soft verging on bottomless over hurdles. The reason is that hurdle races are run on the Flat track, which is extensively watered during the summer. It is not a satisfactory arrangement and the ground can take a great deal out of young hurdlers, not least because this is one of the few courses on which there are more hurdles in the home straight (four) than fences (three). On deep ground, it can be impossible to pick the winner of a hurdle race as they turn into the straight, because some of the leaders will inevitably empty on what can seem an interminable home run.

Few jockeys will enthuse about Leicester. It is approached

through one of the poorer parts of the city, past boarded-up houses and shops, and the course itself is depressing - especially in the rain that seems inevitable at a Leicester meeting. The weighing-room, though relatively new, is a prime example of poor planning. It is far too small and the sauna, which might accommodate eight Flat jockeys, is only big enough for three of my size. RATING: 5

LINGFIELD PARK: There is regrettably little call for me to visit Lingfield these days. It is essentially an all-weather venue now and, while there must be compelling commercial reasons for this, it is a huge shame for everyone who used to enjoy it as the best jumping track south of Sandown. The three National Hunt days retained by Lingfield are not much more than tokenism but so long as the track remains in place I suppose there must be some hope that jumping will be properly revived. I think I speak for all jockeys in saying it would be welcomed, because Lingfield was always in a different league to its nearest neighbours such as Folkestone and Plumpton.

There is so much all-weather racing here now - sometimes up to three days a week - that the sense of raceday occasion has gone. Barely a few hundred turn up for a product that is unashamedly aimed at the betting shops but the knock-on effect is that even the turf meetings here fail to attract a decent crowd. It feels echoingly empty, which is a great pity for a course with fine facilities both for public and jockeys. The weighing-room is pretty faultless and I have a savoury memory of the toasted sandwiches in the tea-room.

It is an undulating track for galloping types. There is plenty of time to ride a tactical race and the fences, though big, are well-made and inviting. One of my first winners here was for the late Captain Tim Forster and if he sent horses to a track on a regular basis you knew it was a venue for proper steeplechasers. There is a sharpish descent before the turn into the home straight and the Flat jockeys seem to compare it with Epsom - so far as I am concerned, it is not a problem as the cambers are good and there is nothing to jump on the way down. Compared to Towcester or Carlisle, it is nothing.

The ground does not drain well and can get very heavy in the winter. I understand the Arena management is doing some work on this now and I can only hope they will put the improved drainage to good use by bringing back jump racing on a serious basis. RATING: 4

LUDLOW: I sometimes think I am the only jockey who likes Ludlow. I sit there some days, in its simple, Hereford-clone of a weighing-room, listening to endless moans about firm ground, bad horses, rogue fences and road crossings and wonder why I am so happy to be there. I suppose it is down to the usual selfish priority of any jockey, which is the chance to ride winners. Most of my Ludlow rides come from the yards of Henry Daly - who trains just up the road - and Philip Hobbs and they tend to be horses that are better than the average for the course. Hence, I have been top jockey for the season two or three times and I am always happy to be back.

It is not a small course but it does have sharp bends, especially over fences, and it certainly suits front-runners. Even a tired horse that is still in front at the second-last will have a good chance of lasting home here, because the track is so flat and undemanding. Specialist two-milers tend to stay two-and-a-half without great difficulty and, as a jockey, two things are paramount. You must never be far off the pacemakers from halfway down the back straight and you must look to pinch some vital lengths round the bends.

The road crossings - four of them in all - are an irritant but I cannot recall horses being seriously inconvenienced or injured by them. As for the prevailing going, you would have to be a complete fool to take a horse to Ludlow that wanted soft ground - other than through a freakish storm just before racing, it never applies. By contrast, in a wet winter (and we seem to have had several recently) it is a haven for trainers with horses crying out for better ground. There was some adverse publicity recently over the first fence in the home straight claiming more than its share of fallers, largely because it was too close to the bend and horses were unbalanced as they jumped it. To their credit, the course management consulted the jockeys before moving it ten yards forward and a shade wider of the rail. Since then, there have been very few casualties and the change can be held up as an example of a course listening to those who actually have to ride round it.

Ludlow is one of the few tracks that has its business areas, by which I mean the weighing-room and paddock, in centre-course. I think it works well and that most spectators quite enjoy trekking across the course to look at the horses before returning to the stands. All in all, this is one of the loveliest places in the country to watch racing but jockeys do not tend to notice such things. They only care about winners. RATING: 7

MARKET RASEN: They still race most months of the year at Market Rasen but I see it as a prime example of a track that has reinvented itself by focussing on summer jumping. There is a very valuable steeplechase here in July (something that would have been unthinkable until recently) and if the concept is judged on attendances it is an outstanding success. The summer crowds at 'Rasen' can be massive and I could see a profitable future for the course in staging two-day fixtures over Saturday and Sunday maybe three times a summer. I am sure such racing weekends would attract a lot of jumping people to an area that is not exactly over-endowed with great sporting events. It might be argued, indeed, that most people would never have heard of Market Rasen but for its racecourse.

The pre-requisite for tracks staging summer jumping is care of the ground and, here, it is kept in very good order. It is a fast course, ten furlongs round, and the third-last fence, which is taken downhill with horses freewheeling towards the straight, will invariably catch somebody out.

For me, the downside to a day in Lincolnshire is that it is a long journey, the latter part of it on fairly slow roads. The car park also becomes a caravan park during the summer, which may have to be sorted out if the racing concentration is to grow, and my gripes inside the course concern a weighing-room that is too cramped and food that relies rather too much on chips and gravy - hardly ideal for jockeys in the middle of any meeting, let alone in the heat of July. Generally, though, I like the course and admire it for its enterprise in changing direction and creating a new and valuable market. RATING: 5

MUSSELBURGH: I might only go to Musselburgh twice a year but each time I ride there I am impressed by the innovations. The investment has been constant in recent years and apart from building an outstanding new weighing-room that could be the model for all aspiring small courses, they have flanked it with a striking entrance hall and modern cafe that can hardly fail to impress the casual racegoer. Not course can have the funds that have clearly been made available here but Musselburgh's management has prioritised sensibly and they deserve to reap the benefits through increased crowds and sponsorship.

The hard work of those running the show can do nothing about the layout of this seaside track, which is arguably its greatest drawback. It is not a nice track to ride round because it is flat, tight and very quick. They go faster round here than anywhere else in the north (where races are commonly run a little slower than at southern tracks) and the feel it gives me is very similar to Taunton.

Benign weather here helps them maintain good ground and trainers despairing of a decent surface elsewhere will often undertake a long journey to Musselburgh for the virtual guarantee it provides. Just such an occasion, a few years back, saw Philip Hobbs send What's Up Boys the vast distance from north Somerset for a novice chase. We were not aware at the time that it was to turn out a hot contest - Frenchman's Creek, an impressive Cheltenham Festival winner in 2002, also ran and fell at the last - but the grey horse did make the journey worthwhile by winning.

One thing that puzzles me about this course is the name it chooses to go by. Until fairly recently, it was known as Edinburgh, which not only bestowed a certain prestige but also, surely, identified it much more accessibly to the majority. Musselburgh is actually a suburb of the city, six miles east of the centre, but I don't follow the logic of renaming the track. RATING: 4

NEWBURY: A jockey struggles to find many excuses around Newbury. It is a wide, galloping track, almost two miles round and with a generous straight that urges you to take your time, never rush. I sometimes think that an idiot could ride round here blindfold, it is so straightforward. The fences down the back straight, though challenging in size, are well-presented and in a straight line, so an experienced jockey can ride a good jumper on autopilot. The joy of the place is in the horses it attracts rather than the curiosities of the course. There are times when the looming presence of one or two outstanding contenders can cut the fields up disappointingly but, round here, you might have only six runners in a novice chase but they would all be worth watching.

One of my first winners for David Nicholson was on this track and as it was intriguingly called Musthaveaswig I always wondered (though never dared ask him) if the boss had named it himself. Having had such a great time under his wing, I was also grateful to be on his final winner before retirement, Picketts Piece - as for him, if it couldn't be at Cheltenham I am sure he was delighted it came at Newbury, because he was always extolling the virtues of the place.

To me, it is Worcester (in its pre-Arena heyday) on a grander scale, as good a course for bumper horses and keen young novice hurdlers as it is for aspirant steeplechasers. The water jump is a spectator feature, positioned right in front of the members' stands, and although such obstacles have caused some controversy in recent years I have no objection to them. Touching wood, I have never fallen at one and I've tended to find them more of a boost to the confidence of a struggling horse than a handicap. Towcester used to have a water jump at the bottom of the hill, far away from the stands and completely wasted on the crowd. To me, offering the public something different through a novel jump is a good thing, but for heaven's sake put it somewhere it can be seen.

The great drawback about Newbury used to be getting in and out, especially on Fridays and Saturdays. On Hennessy day, in particular, it was an annual event to see jockeys and trainers puffing into the course either just in time, or in some cases just too late, having abandoned their cars and run the last half-mile or so. While nobody should pretend the problem has gone away, it has been greatly eased by the Newbury bypass.

Inside, the facilities are improving all the time. I can't remember the days before the Berkshire Stand, when things might not have been on quite such a grand scale, but nowadays the weighing-room is as good as they come, with saunas, a tea-room and a separate television room giving it an air of rare luxury. RATING: 8

NEWCASTLE: I was still an amateur when I first went up to Newcastle, which seemed half a world away then, to ride a 17-hands giant of a horse for a small trainer named Cunningham. When we won, Mr Cunningham let me keep the ride for a two-mile race at Aintree over the National fences. My first experience of that daunting course was safe though not exactly memorable - I think there were four runners and although two of them fell I could still only finish second.

This is a big, galloping track, not far short of two miles round, but I have never regarded it as an especially nice place to be riding over fences. Going away from the stands and into the country, a couple of fences are met on a slightly downhill stretch and though they don't look particularly intimidating they seem to produce too many fallers. Even seasoned handicappers can get in trouble there. In general, the track suits big, bold jumpers the best and the half-mile long home straight, rising steadily, finds out any deficiencies of stamina. I enjoy riding the hurdles course, as the sweeping back straight, set on a slight curve, allows you to give a young horse plenty of time and still have the scope to challenge after the home turn.

Sir Stanley Clarke and his Northern Racing group have made

gradual changes since taking over at Gosforth Park and there is no doubt it has the standing of one of the premier tracks in the north. Set against that, it has dour stone buildings and a very dated weighing-room which is inclined to feel very cold in winter. The amenities work, though, and the food - once pretty dire - is slowly improving. The same cannot be said with certainty about the state of the ground, which was little short of disgraceful at one recent spring meeting. It led to a flood of withdrawn horses and a shared sense of grievance among the trainers who had taken horses up there and the jockeys who had travelled to ride them. Scant effort appeared to have been made on areas of the track that were simply rough and the groundstaff there must beware a bad reputation - it is an unavoidable fact that if you produce unacceptable ground once in 20 meetings, people will remember that far more readily than they recall the other 19. RATING: 5

NEWTON ABBOT: I used to hate going to this course just outside the Torbay holiday area. It wasn't the problem of dodging caravans and open-top cars that put me off but the quality of horses I had to ride. Usually, I was confined to partnering obscure creatures for permit holders whose names my agent, Dave Roberts, had managed to find under a filing cabinet. My arrangement with Philip Hobbs has transformed all that, though, and like the other west-country tracks this is now a profitable place for me.

If a trainer has a decent horse that has lost his confidence, this is an ideal course to help restore it. By contrast, a genuinely suspect jumper should avoid the place, because the fences are frequent and mistakes can cost you dear. It might sound odd but is actually easier to ride such horses at Wetherby or Newbury, where the fences are bigger but they have loads of time and space to put themselves right.

Like Market Rasen, Newton Abbot is directing much of its promotional attention towards summer jumping now, with 11 racedays between mid-June and the end of August. Positioned as it is, so close to so many holidaymakers, it makes perfect sense and the groundstaff has been playing its part in keeping the ground decent through watering over the last two summers. Increased prize money and crowd levels have already resulted but from a jockey's viewpoint, the opening of the new weighing-room was a key moment. As the old one was like a garden shed they could hardly do other than improve. RATING: 6

PERTH: Even for jockeys consumed by the pursuit of winners, there are certain racecourses that are anticipated with relish no matter the quality of racing. Perth ranks high among them. It is a simple, unexceptional track and, as the most northerly venue in the country, it is a long way from home for the majority. No matter. Once there, even the most cynical can be won over by the atmosphere of a course at which everyone seems to be having fun. The mood is dictated from the top, as the clerk of the course Sam Morshead spends much of his time organising nightly parties for everyone. I sometimes think Sam must have taken far too many bangs on the head during his years as a jump jockey but for all his eccentricity he is the ideal man to be running a course like Perth.

It is at its best in April, when the annual three-day festival takes place. Considering the distances involved, a surprising number of leading southern trainers, such as Nigel Twiston-Davies, Kim Bailey and Philip Hobbs, send up box-loads of runners for this meeting. The prize money is relatively good but I suspect the trainers enjoy stopping up in this lovely part of Scotland for three days, too. Unsurprisingly, one-day fixtures never work quite so well here, certainly so far as the southern jockeys and trainers are concerned - those who are more local may actually breathe a sigh of relief.

The track is flat and fast and the ground can vary hugely from day to day, because it dries so fast yet is also next to a river and prone to flooding. One April, the first day of the festival rode good, the next day it was heavy and the third day was abandoned for waterlogging. Two seasons in succession the entire festival was lost to freakish rain, a huge blow not just to the course but to the friendly town, which thrives during race week.

The fences here have usually been good but standards slipped last season when they had what we call a lack of belly. Put simply, this means that they appear to dip rather than swell in the middle, a fault that can encourage horses to get into the bottom of them. Typical of Perth, though, everyone was very obliging when it was drawn to their attention and normal service was quickly resumed. Recently, they have revamped the weighing-room, making it slightly bigger and installing a decent sauna. The showers never used to work here but the last time I went they had three in full working order. Sadly, the same applied to the bagpipes which traditionally accompany us to the paddock prior to the first race. Some jockeys claim to enjoy it because they can't hear their instructions from the trainer. RATING: 6

PLUMPTON: This is one of the worst tracks in the country. It stages a lot of racing through the winter months and the management deserve some credit for keeping it on at times, but the fact remains that the ground is often bottomless until spring, when the drying process leaves it hard and rough. Turf maintenance cannot be easy but the outcome of the conditions is that very few jockeys enjoy riding here.

Fred Winter, I understand, refused to ride over the Plumpton fences. Most of us are not in the exalted position to take such a decision, though many might like to. There are two particularly problematic fences at the foot of the plunging hill that comprises the back straight and it is here that problems occur most frequently. Moderate horses, freewheeling down the hill, are racing in earnest and unable to cope with the drops.

The hurdles track is also fast and furious and the novice events, generally of a modest standard, tend to attract one or two horses of obviously better quality, sent here to pick up an easy win. Martin Pipe, who has more firepower than anyone, sends plenty down this route.

Facilities for the riders are very similar to Folkestone and Fontwell, with a couple of interesting variations. The weighing-room here is also used as a gym and although they shift the equipment to one side on racedays, the space is compromised. The tea-room is run by a Spaniard named Caesar, who spends the day laughing uproariously at everything we say - something, at least, to raise the spirits. RATING: 2

SANDOWN PARK: The chase course is the thing here - probably one of the finest racing spectacles Britain has to offer. There are seven fences down the back straight - two plain ones, then a ditch and then a water jump (too far from the stands to mean anything) before drawing breath for the crux of the race, the three closely sited Railway fences. There is a great deal of talk about how best to ride these obstacles and it is true they are as close as we come to an event course. For me, though, you can't be counting strides in a steeplechase and you must never be worrying about the third of these fences while jumping the first - that is asking for trouble. A good jockey will jump the fences as they come and simply concentrate on putting his horse right at each one. Time after time, the Railway section will change the shape of a race, eliminating one or two contenders either by falls or mistakes, but there is then a long, sweeping run round the last bend before the Pond fence. This is something of a confidence restorer, a nice fence to jump, but it is also the place where you can usually identify the potential winner travelling better than anything else.

The same is not often true of the second-last hurdle. They use the flat course for hurdle races and the ground is usually softer than on the chase course. Races can be run at a searching gallop and it can be a demanding slog up the final hill, which is far stiffer than most would imagine. If you took a picture at the second-last flight of a handicap hurdle and then looked at the result, you might struggle to believe it - all too often, the horse in front with one more to jump will fade to finish sixth or seventh.

Not so long ago, Sandown lost a sequence of winter meetings through waterlogging. The drainage problems have now been resolved and everyone, from jockeys through to the racing public, should be thankful, for we cannot afford to having meetings needlessly abandoned on such a wonderful track. Apart from the Esher traffic, so horrific that I tend to leave two hours more than the average journey time for a Saturday meeting, I can pick very few holes in this venue. The spectator facilities have recently been lavishly upgraded but jockey amenities have always been first-rate, with a spacious and well-designed weighing-room and excellent food.

The finale meeting at the end of April is an excellent innovation.

Many of us in the business enjoyed the traditional end-of-season weekend at Stratford but the fact is that the general public was never really aware that it represented the changing of seasons. Sandown promote the occasion outstandingly well and the one question to be resolved is whether the two days should remain a combination of flat and jumps races or be split into flat racing on the Friday and an entirely jumping card on Saturday. Jockeys, enjoying the rare opportunity to mix, would probably opt to keep things as they are but I can see the commercial argument for making the Saturday card a full-scale jumping finale. The one thing I would ask is that the race we still call the Whitbread (now the Attheraces Gold Cup) should formally close the season for professional jockeys. If they have to run a couple of races afterwards, follow the lead of Aintree on National day and close with a hunter chase and a bumper. The Whitbread is a natural point of closure and it feels artificial to be going out for another, lesser race afterwards. RATING: 8

SEDGEFIELD: The distance is a deterrent and it is not the most memorable place when you get there, but Sedgefield has been kind to me over the years, so I have a spot in my heart for it. Especially kind, in fact, during the autumn of 1995, when I was an aspirant amateur - desperate for rides with any kind of chance - and Peter Bowen was fresh into training from the point-to-point ranks. Peter had an ex-Irish staying chaser called Iffeee and he asked me to go up to ride it in a 3m3f race at Sedgefield. It was a Monday in early October and I diffidently asked David Nicholson if I could leave after first lot. He was instinctively brusque about it, demanding to know why I was going 'all the way up there' for one dodgy ride. He had not often been to Sedgefield himself and I don't suppose he knew much about P.Bowen, so he looked at me with a pitying scorn as I set off. The horse won at 20-1 and although I got some good publicity from the ride it did me more good back at home, with the Duke beginning to view my outings north for Peter Bowen with more interest. Iffeee ran at Sedgefield again three weeks later, this time sent off favourite, and we made all for another win. Good memories, then, even if my first impression of the track was not exactly starstruck. It rode like a northern version of Plumpton and, in fact, it does a very similar job, providing low-grade racing on Mondays and Tuesdays to keep the betting pool active and offer opportunities for horses (and jockeys) that might otherwise struggle. It served a purpose.

The chase track looks as if it is on the turn all the time but actually rides better than it looks. There is a very sharp bend out of the back straight, though, and the fence at the top of the downhill straight is often dolled off in bad weather, which is a relief to all as it can be a pig. It is quite steeply downhill after that and the ground falls away at the last fence, often catching out the tired and unwary. You need a quick, nimble horse round here and many of the regular chasers look more like flat horses. The ground gets a hammering from a heavy diet of midwinter racing. It can sometimes get loose and the bends are often more brown than green.

It would not be a favourite track even to northern jockeys, let alone those of us for whom it is a half-day hike away, but it is a very friendly spot, peopled by some wizened old characters that you see at meeting. There is a recently built weighing-room, very well designed, and I have no doubt the facilities will continue to get better now that Sir Stanley Clarke has added it to his swelling empire. One area that certainly needs attention is the jockeys' catering, which still errs on the meat pie side of sensible.

RATING: 4

SOUTHWELL: I am not sorry to have missed the brief and ill-fated experiment with jump racing on all-weather tracks. It never sounded a good idea to me and the statistics of fallers and injured horses are quite sufficient to persuade me it should never be revived. At Southwell, which shared the stage with Lingfield, the legacy lives on, though, because the new configuration of the all-weather track (still used for interminable days of soulless flat racing) means that the turf track inside it is one of the sharpest in the country at barely a mile round. They use portable fences here, which are not especially well-made and probably too big for the size of the track and the standard of horses. Hence, they get a lot of falls.

Thankfully, I took no part in the notorious race in 2001-2 when the entire field came to grief, some of them more than once, before A.P.McCoy predictably remounted to steal the winner. Bizarre though it was, it did not entirely surprise me - it was an accident waiting to happen. Some years back, I rode in a five-runner novice chase there for David Nicholson and fell down the back straight. By then, two of the others had already come down and so, with only two possible rivals left, I decided to remount for the first time in my career. There was another casualty and I did complete safely to finish second but 'The Duke' was not happy. He is very much of the 'never remount' school of thinking and, with hindsight, I pretty much agree with him. My horse was standing compliantly next to me in this instance but it is true that you cannot be sure if they have been injured by the original fall.

Southwell's hurdles course, on which they use the French-style brush obstacles, is fine and they do make a big effort to keep the summer jumping ground well watered. The facilities are adequate - certainly no better than that - but there is always an echoing, empty atmosphere simply through the lack of a proper crowd. I'm told it is even sparser on flat racing days, so I suppose we are lucky. Where we are not lucky, though, is in literally picking up the leftovers from the flat-race jockeys, who must carry a fair proportion of the track back in with them after each race. No matter how much they might brush the weighing-room floor it appears to make no difference and I have always gone home from here with an irritating amount of sand in my shoes and the feeling that I'm in need of a second shower. My philosophy is to go anywhere if there is the chance of a winner - but Southwell would be very low on my list. RATING: 3.

STRATFORD: To many people, Stratford may rate no higher than the Plumptons and Sedgefields of the circuit but to me it is in a different league. It may not be the greatest track to ride round - it is always on the turn, especially over hurdles, and you can be very unlucky here without making a riding mistake - but I love the place because I have always gone there with decent chances. Shallow, maybe, but it is what makes a jockey happy.

When David Nicholson was training, 40 minutes' drive away, he would always run better than average horses at Stratford. The same is now true of Alan King, Philip Hobbs and Henry Daly, so I am thrice blessed. The racing here can be mighty competitive, especially during May when some useful horses are trying to pick up a win or two before being put out in a field for the summer, and the atmosphere of these meetings is always very good. They race a lot on Friday evenings, while the two-day meeting at the end of May traditionally marked the end of the season until the switch was made to Sandown a month earlier. When I was working for 'The Duke', I used to go to the Friday night meetings even if I wasn't riding - there would always be a lot of local people I knew at the track, and a casual, shirtsleeve atmosphere. It is the only racecourse I've ever seen 'The Duke' without a tie.

Sensibly, Stratford concentrates on its summer programme now and the ground is looked after very well. Eric, the groundsman, tends to come in the weighing-room before racing for a chat with the jockeys and he has gained their respect - no easy thing, as he had to follow Reg Lomas in the job, and Reg was the best groundsman most of us have known. What he doesn't know about turf, and indeed fence-building, is not worth knowing, and I was delighted when Cheltenham took him on for a few years after he was retired too early by Stratford. In my view, the Jockey Club should be enlisting the help of people like Reg to instruct new groundsmen; certainly, his talent is precious to our sport and should not be wasted.

Stratford has only one entrance, which makes it a bottleneck on the busy days, and some of its facilities still leave a bit to be desired. The weighing-room is hidden away underneath the old stand. It feels as if it is underground - a bit dark, a bit cold in winter but pleasantly cool on the hot summer afternoons. The showers are poor but there is a decent sauna and the great bonus of food by Matt - this is where he started his tearoom operation. RATING: 7

TAUNTON: My biggest complaint about Taunton is that, even as jockeys, we struggle to get in and struggle to get out. Getting away is difficult because of the narrow road that services the track - many is the time I have longed for them to build an extra exit off the M5, just for racedays - but the entrance problem is down to the officious gatemen. Jockeys are issued with swipe cards these days and we are supposed to show them at the gate each day. I confess I never have mine to hand - it is usually left in the car - and despite the fact that I have a bag over my shoulder with my name on it, and the same gatemen have been seeing me arrive to ride at meeting for some years now, they still get their jobsworth hats on and make life difficult. Other tracks have been similar in the past - Hereford was notorious at one time - but Taunton is now the worst case.

If this has not put me into too sour a mood at the start of a day, I tend to enjoy Taunton. As usual, it is down to opportunity - this is a local track for Philip Hobbs, so I normally go there with a few chances. Sadly, of course, it is also THE local track for Martin Pipe, which usually means that A.P.'s odds-on shots comfortably outnumber mine. The first decent day I had at Taunton, though, actually involved a double for a small trainer named Gordon Edwards. I'm not sure who was the more surprised - Gordon or me. One of the horses was Chickabiddy, who, by coincidence, also provided A.P.McCoy with his first British winner.

The ground used to be bad. Indeed, it was sometimes hard here, before that description was rightly banned and before watering systems became more widespread and effective. It rides much better now but there are still some notorious hazards on the steeplechase course to overcome. The first fence in the home straight causes plenty of falls, with horses tending to run into the bottom of it, and speed causes plenty of casualties at the first in the back, which comes quickly after the bend. Unusually, for a small course, there are also two open ditches in the back straight, which caused me no end of concern when Philip entered Atavistic to run there. For some reason, this horse just dreads open ditches - I think he is simply scared of them - and I spent the journey down wondering how to ride him. It was my lucky day. The clerk of the course marched into the weighing-room before racing to tell us that two fences had been dolled off due to bad ground - it happened to be both of the ditches. Atavistic won, too, so this could be put down as a clever piece of placement by P.Hobbs. He was probably not congratulating himself so much the day a decent grey horse was beaten here in his first novice chase - a result that seems all the stranger now, as his name is What's Up Boys.

Jockey facilities are fairly primitive, although the sauna is a recent addition and they have given the weighing-room a lick of fresh paint. The food has been done for years by the same two old boys and is not memorable. RATING: 6

TOWCESTER: Those who ride - or simply watch their racing - in America, where all the tracks are flat, left-handed clones of one another, would be baffled by a course like Towcester. It is right-handed, for one thing, but it is also set on the side of a hill and you are constantly going either up or down it. It demands a particular type of horse, especially when the ground is testing, as it often is in mid-winter. When looking at a Towcester card, it is always worth following a horse that has won here before - if the horse you are considering has done all his winning at tracks like Ludlow or Taunton, forget it.

The hill in the home straight is probably the stiffest climb in the country and it is on you very quickly, draining the reserves from many horses. I remember going there on a Bank Holiday last year thinking one of my rides simply couldn't get beaten, but he just didn't handle the track. Many horses stop to virtually nothing up the hill, having turned in apparently still cruising - time after time, you could stop the film of a race at the bottom of the hill and completely fail to spot the eventual winner. One odd thing is that riding round here tends to tire a jockey less than on quick, flat tracks. If you are on a horse that handles the hills he will probably carry you through; if you are not, the chances are you will pull up.

Towcester has one of the worst fences in the country for fallers. It is taken downhill at the start of the three-mile chase course and it can feel like jumping into mid-air. There are often a lot of runners in chases here (trainers like Henry Daly love it) and there is such a cavalry charge to the first that it is often jumped too fast, with the result that unbalanced horses stumble as they land.

Towcester is a well-sited course, convenient for the M1 and the M40, and the new road now being built past Silverstone will make it even more accessible. The management has plenty of work to do, following the compulsory demolition of the condemned main stand, and I just hope that the construction of a new one will include a modernised weighing-room. At present, we change on ancient wooden benches in what might kindly be described as an old potting shed - recently repainted but otherwise unaltered, probably for generations. The winners' enclosure, directly outside, is also very small and old-fashioned, reminiscent of a point-to-point. This is a lovely old course, very popular with many people, but I think it needs to take a few steps forward. RATING: 5

UTTOXETER: As a boy, I would have had no idea what part of the country Uttoxeter was in but I did know it had a racecourse - quite an important one to me, because it was here that Dad rode Bridge Ash to win the Midlands Grand National, the biggest win of his riding career and the start of a Johnson family dynasty with the 'Bridge' progeny. In those days, Uttoxeter was still very much a rural, farmers' track but since it became the first and flagship course for Stan Clarke's management style it has changed out of all recognition and become so popular it is now a victim of its own success. Midlands National day in 2002 came, as it often does, at the end of Cheltenham week and although I got there early enough to get a decent parking slot, I decided to recharge from an energy-sapping week with an extra hour's sleep in the car. When I woke, still more than an hour before the first race, I was surrounded by a sea of cars and people. The crowds here are good even for the ordinary cards; on the big days there is just not enough room for everyone to be comfortable and there seems little chance of further expansion as there is a busy railway line directly behind the stand.

They stage some very valuable races here each season now, not only during the winter but also in late June, when their summer National, worth £50,000, gives a decent opportunity for the fast-ground chasers to earn some serious money. I like racing here in the summer and seriously wonder if they should begin to think of a midwinter break. At present, this is the only jumping track in the country to race in all 12 months of the year and it does, inevitably, have a detrimental effect on the track. It does not cope well with excesses of rain and, as there is no real recovery time, the ground gets very chewed up.

The track is an odd shape, with a dog-leg on the back straight. It rides well enough, and with four fences in the home straight there is plenty of time to ride a proper race, yet for some reason we often go too fast here on soft ground and you will see too many Uttoxeter chases with only two or three finishers.

They have done wonders with the traffic system, which was a high priority considering the volume of cars that descend on an otherwise nondescript town, and if you know the country road that drops you straight onto the racecourse roundabout it is a doddle.

Facilities inside have been greatly enhanced for the public and although the weighing-room is a bit of a prefab it is well-designed and contains everything we need. In time, knowing the drive and initiative of Sir Stanley, I would be surprised if they don't build something grander. RATING: 6

WARWICK: Good and bad here, but in my view the good wins through. Much the most impressive thing about Warwick is that it is aggressively forward-thinking, scared of no other track in its bid to make progress up the ladder. There was a Saturday last winter when it outshone Ascot for prize money, top jockeys and good horses - even a year or two earlier that would have been unthinkable. It's all down to lively management at a course where the clerk is now my old riding colleague and near neighbour Robert Bellamy. 'Bells' was always one of the good guys of the weighing-room and he has made an immediate impression in his new job.

The track is another of those English eccentricities, because it disappears behind a hill for half-a-mile and I would not care to think of the tricks that were pulled round there before the days of vigilant patrol cameras. No obstacles are jumped on that stretch but when the runners emerge into view on the back straight five fences come in quick succession. This is not only a decent spectacle for those in the stands but a very good test of jumping ability - a proficient jumper can win round here even if he is not the quickest horse in the race. Trainers seem to like running good horses at Warwick and its racing has become ever more competitive in recent seasons. My one concern would be that the frequency of racing here means that the track takes a lot of hammer - the ground has occasionally been criticised and I would hate to see it get the kind of reputation that will deter trainers from running anything decent.

They have done a great job of revamping the main stand but there is a fair way to go before the management can pat itself on the back about the overall standard of facilities. The car park is a field that becomes a bog in wet weather - it needs surfacing. The weighing-room is extremely old and small. Ideally, it needs burning down. RATING: 7.

WETHERBY: My good memories here stretch back to winning a valuable novice chase on Mr Mulligan, the year before his Gold Cup glory, and to taking the Christmas feature, the Castleford Chase, on the great Viking Flagship for David Nicholson. In those days, though the track itself was virtually as it is now, the facilities for public and jockeys were vastly different. In recent years they have built a glitzy new stand, with stylish restaurants, bars and boxes, and matched it with a brilliant weighing-room and office block that overlooks the paddock. The layout is very effective and Wetherby seem to have got everything right with the scope and design of their amenities - it makes me wonder how other courses can get such developments so badly wrong.

Being right next to the A1, Wetherby has always had plenty going for it but there is a sense of purposeful management now, of a course very much on the up. The racing is invariably of good class here, which is entirely due to the quality of the track itself. In the north of the country, only Haydock can rival it. If I was a trainer, heaven forbid, I would not be scared of taking a moderate jumper to Wetherby, because this is such a broad, galloping track that there is absolutely no rush and a horse can be coaxed around in his own time, usually without being taken off his feet.

The fences used to be notoriously massive and I remember, in my early days at Jackdaws Castle, that Barton Bank was dispatched to

Wetherby and came back after the indignity of a fall. They have been modified considerably since then and now ride very well, one more sign of an exemplary course that I always look forward to riding. RATING: 8

WINCANTON: Always popular and effectively promoted, Wincanton is like a huge point-to-point for professionals. It just has that feel about it, doubtless because it is apparently sited in the middle of nowhere. I used to get lost time every time I drove there alone and although I now know the way well enough, there are so many different routes through the lanes of rural Somerset. For all that, it is a spruce, well cared-for course, with a neat, well-sited weighing-room and adequate facilities. Nobody in authority can be blamed for its main drawback - wind.

The track is set on top of a hill and seems to attract every passing breath of wind. In winter, it invariably slices through you, leaving you feeling unpleasantly cold after a day's riding. Wind is not, in itself, a hazard to riding although I have come across a few horses that don't like it - Needwood Lion, one of Henry Daly's, just goes silly in high wind and becomes a real handful.

A product of the wind is dry ground. Even in midwinter, horses are sent to Wincanton in search of fast ground and anyone complaining about it being quick in May needs to have a better look at the form book. As a jockey, you cannot afford to drop far off the pace round here and I thought the performance of Looks Like Trouble, in winning over an utterly inadequate 2m5f last January, was one of the best I have seen.

The fences here used to be poorly made - too stiff and upright, guaranteeing a crop of mistakes and falls - but in the past two years they have improved considerably. The hurdles course is not so good. The obstacles themselves are sometimes like gates, very un-inviting for a young horse, and the one taken running away from the winning post, past the stables, is in such a dip that it disorientates many horses. RATING: 5

WOLVERHAMPTON: My instincts are very protective towards the volume and variety of British racecourses but I make an exception here - Wolverhampton should be shut down as a National Hunt course and left to concentrate on the floodlit, dirt-track flat fare that is its staple output.

It cannot be disputed that facilities here have improved greatly since Arena Leisure bought the course. The access roads are now very good, there is a vast tarmac car park, a hotel on site and a 400-seater viewing restaurant which, I'm told, is booked out weeks ahead for the Saturday night meetings. Arena smartly hit on a product that no-one else is offering - not yet, anyway - and are reaping the benefits. But I can't help wishing they had built their floodlit track somewhere else (say, on the still unused site of the long abandoned Birmingham racecourse, to the west of the M6) and left Wolverhampton to the jumping fraternity who always had such affection for it.

I led up a horse there for my grandad. I was 14 years old and it was to be my only visit before the old jumps track was shut and building work left the site unrecognisable. Both my family and David Nicholson had been very fond of the old course, and the Duke had sent a lot of his good horses there, praising its broad, galloping characteristics. He still bemoans its loss today and points out that jump racing has been equally ill-served by the decisions of Nottingham and Windsor to race exclusively on the flat.

When Wolverhampton re-opened, the turf course was an

afterthought. For a time, it rode like it, too - the surface was very poor. It can still be patchy, especially when watered, but is slowly improving. The track, though, is tight and unwelcoming and the fences are far too upright for its shape. If they are to persevere with jumping here, it would be better to stage all-hurdles cards, for which they should be guaranteed plenty of runners. My overriding feeling, though, is that jump racing to Wolverhampton is tokenism, a pure irrelevance. To someone like me, this is a decent track wrecked. RATING: 2

WORCESTER: Arena Leisure is also the management company for Worcester and they have a fair bit to answer for here, too. Worcester, alongside the river in a lovely old town, has one of the best settings in the country and, properly promoted, could surely be a thriving racecourse. Instead, its ground is unreliable and its facilities are little short of a disgrace. It does not stop me liking the place, partly because it is local and dear to my heart but largely for the scope of the track and the potential for better things. Like others in racing, though, I am suspicious about the motives of the management, who promised to rebuild the stands and the weighing-room but have so far achieved very little. Rumours about their plans are ten-a-penny but if they ever turned this place into another Wolverhampton it would be a shameful act for which the racing community would never forgive them.

Of course, Worcester is not an entirely straightforward track to administer - the river, pretty though it is, complicates matters. It floods in winter and nobody can do anything about that. Arena has already taken a sensible step in switching Worcester's fixtures to the summer. Watering must be simple here and the ground should now be ideal, yet somehow it is worse than it ever was when they held racing here through the winter. Can somebody explain that? Reg Lomas probably could, and I expect he could do something to improve the situation very quickly. Worcester could do a lot worse than call him in. At present, trainers are in danger of losing confidence - and, when that happens, the track struggles to recover.

So much more could be made of this place. The track is like Newbury on a country scale - similar size and with no hidden worries for horse or jockey, a delight to ride round. With the attraction of the situation, this should be the flagship course for summer jumping and could profitably stage a three-day festival when the weather is at its best. If Warwick, which is far from attractive, can perform such wonders with its prize money I cannot see why Worcester should be languishing behind and the best of the summer horses could be gathered here to grab some attention for jumping.

I honestly don't think this is an idle pipedream but when I look at the state of Worcester now I wonder if it will ever come about. The main stand is shocking and the weighing-room is just waiting to fall over. It is tiny inside, with a new sauna the one blessing - and so decrepit I am amazed it hasn't been condemned. It is built on brick stilts, right by the riverside. One day, maybe, it will fall in and do us all a favour. RATING: 6

18.

A royal relationship

On the day before the 2002 Cheltenham Festival was due to start, one of the tabloid papers ran a story claiming I was about to get married. It was pure invention, fanciful nonsense, and a year or so earlier I would have been outraged by the cheek of it. Now, I just laughed and wondered what they would come up with next. It was so predictable, really. It was a huge week for horse racing, one of the few weeks in the year when the sport grabs an audience outside its own circles, so the gossip writers had to make up something appropriate. Is that a cynical view? I don't think so. After a while, it becomes easier to see through such shallow thinking. I know now, you see, that with a royal girlfriend, such mischief-making comes with the territory.

Of course, it was obvious that my social life was destined for some changes once I started going out with Zara Phillips but at first I gave it very little thought. The fact was that we had met in a racing environment and shared plenty of the same friends and boltholes. We were both living in the Cotswolds, albeit at different ends of the area, and we had met up socially even before there was anything between us. So it was not as if I suddenly started to think there were places we should not go or people we should not talk to. For me, such worries only imposed themselves after we had decided to go our separate ways.

We broke up in mid-July of 2002. We had been together for more than two years and I like to think it had been a good time in both our lives but, even when we split, Zara was only 21 and I was 24. We both had busy lives and there was a lot of living still to do. Parting is never easy, seldom entirely without upset, but there was no acrimony, no lasting damage and no third party on either side. We had a relationship and we moved on. Young people like us do it all the time and nobody passes comment.

I knew, of course, that we were never going to be treated with such courtesy but, even allowing for the inevitable media attention for which the preceding two years had prepared me well, I was shocked by the persistent fabrications of certain tabloid papers who seemed intent on creating a racier story than actually existed. In their methods and perseverence, they made my life miserable for several weeks, as each morning renewed the paranoia of wondering what nonsense they would publish next.

They did not just pursue me, they pursued my friends, close and casual. Reporters followed me around some of the more isolated racecourses - one newspaper even sent two journalists to Sedgefield - and they were certainly not there to write about the outcome of the novice chase. For some days, there were press cars at the end of my drive and one report claimed that my lawn was overgrown and I had dirty dishes in my sink. Leaving aside the moral issue of the snooping necessary to claim such facts, they were simply untrue - I had cut the lawn myself a few days earlier and my newly appointed cleaner had left the kitchen spotless.

Countless calls came into my mobile phone - the number of which is published in all racing guides - from people who either introduced themselves as journalists or unsuccessfully pretended not to be. I said nothing, on the basis that anything I did say could be taken out of context and the last thing I wanted was to cause any further upset for Zara or her family. For some days, though, I felt so harried I did not answer the phone.

Some papers, it seemed, were determined to paint me as the bad guy, no matter how far they had to bend the truth to do so. I was waiting for them to come up with some person who had allegedly broken us up and, sure enough, it happened. The chosen individual was Jonjo O'Neill's daughter, Louise. I had met her three times in large groups of people, on the last occasion at my 25th birthday party, a week after Zara and I had parted. We were not together in any sense but three weeks later (three weeks in which I did not even see her) some papers were still writing of us as if we were now an item and doubtless due for imminent wedding bells. Sometimes it made me laugh. Sometimes it made me angry. It was an unsettling period but, ironically, it reinforced my admiration for the royal family and my sympathy for what they, and other high-profile people, have to endure on a regular basis.

The earliest bond between Zara and me was a shared love of horses. With Zara's increasingly competitive eventing, and her interests in racing, that mutual interest remained as strong as ever through the time we were together, though both of us acknowledged the commitment that the other had to put into the chosen sport. Success does not just happen, for royalty or for anyone else, and eventually it was the growing awareness that we both had careers to pursue that did as much as anything else to make us think that our relationship might have run its course.

It so happened that in this romance I met the mother before the girl herself. The Princess Royal had kept a couple of horses at David Nicholson's yard and had ridden out there regularly even before I started working for the Duke. Gatcombe, their home, was an easy drive from Jackdaws Castle and, eventually, the Princess started bringing Zara to ride out on one of the old horses in the yard. There was never much opportunity for conversation - they came in for one lot and vanished again, so far as we were concerned - but that did not stop David Barker, the incorrigible 'Scouse', from offering his usual outspoken views to the Princess. He called her 'the old bird', among other things, and, in his engagingly funny way, made it clear that although he was fully aware who she was, he did not see why he should treat her any differently to everyone else. I think this suited her fine and that she actually enjoyed the banter with 'Scouse'. Certainly, she has always been very straight, very down-to-earth, which many people admire in her - and I think those qualities have rubbed off on Zara.

It was still to be quite some time before we started seeing anything of each other. Zara began riding out at Jackdaws more regularly, during her summer holidays from Gordonstoun School, and it was while she was doing her A-levels that we first met up occasionally, though only in a big circle of friends and certainly without any romantic intentions on either part. After finishing school, she went off travelling. While she was experiencing life in the equine communities of New Zealand, spending time in Jamaica and Hawaii, then working for three months in a P.R. agency in Sydney, I was concentrating fully on the opportunities coming my way during the 1999-2000 season. And there were plenty of them. I was 22, riding high in the jockeys' championship and surrounded by a bunch of great friends. I had a good social life, generally among the jockeys with whom I spent my working hours but also back home in Herefordshire, where I would meet up regularly with a lot of long-term mates from boyhood. Life was good and I was

244

not consciously looking for anything more. Then, just before Cheltenham, Zara came home.

We met for a drink once or twice, in one or other of the Cotswold pubs that we both knew. It might have been The Plough, just at the foot of the Jackdaws gallops and the place where, over the years, half an hour of the double act quite naturally performed by Richard Phillips and Gordon Clarkson has given me my fix of entertainment for a week. We both knew them, along with plenty of other racing folk who frequented such pubs. Somehow, though, I must have done something to attract her interest. Straight after Looks Like Trouble won the Gold Cup, the Duke threw a party at his home and Zara and I spent a good bit of the evening chatting. Slightly to my surprise, it went on from there and, within a couple of months, we were going out together properly.

It may seem curious to some people but the fact is I never worried about the royal connection, because I had not met her through that. We had met on the mutual, neutral ground of a racing yard and, because of that, nothing seemed strange about the relationship at all. Zara had always cheerfully joined in the bantering at Jackdaws, giving as good as she got, and I had found her easy to speak to, fun to be around. The best thing about her was a complete absence of pretension.

Not that everyone was likely to regard our going out in such a matter-of-fact way - and, here, I am not referring exclusively to the press. You can't keep news like that quiet in the jockeys' weighing-room, for instance, and several months of relentless ribbing ensued. It was always going to be that way but I think the lads eventually grew tired of it and moved on to something else.

My parents were happy about it, though I'm not sure Dad knew who she was - he's hopeless like that. One day, after we had been back home, Zara and I were in a shop in Hereford when an old lady approached her, gestured in my direction and said, quite innocently: "Doesn't he look like that jockey who's going out with Princess Anne's daughter?" We both agreed, with stoically solemn faces. "And you look a bit like her, too," the lady added. Trying desperately not to laugh, we said there must be an odd likeness and made a rapid escape, leaving the woman looking increasingly quizzical.

For Zara, it is usually not so easy to escape recognition. Until I knew her, I had never appreciated the extent of the paparazzi ordeal. In fact, I had never taken it seriously at all. As a sportsman, I have my picture taken quite regularly, sometimes when I am unprepared and often when I'm not looking my best. I can't say I enjoy it but you just tend to switch off from the process. If I could do it, I thought, why should royals and celebrities be worried about a few clicking cameras? I didn't know the half of it, but I was soon to find out.

One of the first times we went out together in London was to a show - it was the opening night of 'The King and I' and James Erskine, the man Zara had worked for in Sydney, was putting it on. When I say 'together', however, it is not quite true, because I flew back from the Punchestown Festival that evening and it was arranged that I would make my own way to the theatre as soon as possible. Well, I never actually got to see any of the show, as there was less than half-an-hour left when I arrived and I did not feel like making a noisy entrance with everyone gawping at me. I arrived in a black cab, showed my pass at the doors and was shown upstairs to one of the lounges to wait for everyone to come out. As I went in, I noticed a lot of photographers sitting around, taking no interest in me other than a few strange looks regarding my timekeeping. I thought no more about them until the moment when Zara and I, having met up when the curtain came down, emerged to leave the theatre, and all hell broke loose.

The pack of photographers were all there for Zara, and now that they had the bonus of a boyfriend in the picture they were intent on milking the moment. As we walked down this West End street, they were running backwards in front of us, contorting themselves to get the best angles. Some were holding their cameras above their heads and firing randomly. One fell over a dustbin but jumped to his feet with his camera intact and starting running and pointing once more. I was genuinely shocked, and no doubt looked it, but for Zara and her brother, Peter, it was no more or less than they had seen many times before.

There was an element of slapstick comedy to the scene, now that I look back on it, but to be in the midst of it all, a target for the photographic fervour, was an unnerving experience. It was a real eye-opener for me and I realise now that celebrities have to endure this all the time. I feel sorry for them - not just for Zara and her family but for the likes of David Beckham, who cannot do anything in public without the company of intrusive cameramen. I understand, now, how people can be pushed to the limit by this pitiless pressure and how, on occasions, it can lead to verbal or even physical altercations.

That night in London was the first time we had been seen together in such a public environment and, I suppose I realised then that life with Zara was going to have an edge to it and that I must start adjusting to different expectations. The good thing, though, is that we so seldom did anything or went anywhere to attract such attention. I have never been a city person and Zara isn't, either, so we were very rarely out in London as sitting ducks for the paparazzi. We both like the countryside and we both love being at home - and, for some while, home was a shared experience.

Every now and again, it seemed to me, the press got bored and it became Zara's turn to be the subject of the gossip columns or the silly-story syndrome. I realise now that royals and celebrities have to put up with this all the time. I have also come to see, partly through my own subsequent experiences, that so much can be invented, or at least exaggerated in the papers to satisfy the craving for celebrity 'news'. I had always, innocently, tended to believe what I read, just as I am sure many people believed much of what they read about me after our break-up. I am far more cynical about it now. The wedding speculation was an example of that - it wasn't me they were interested in, and I'm not daft enough to think it was. A royal wedding, though, is quite a prospect for the tabloids to get excited about - well, it would have been if it was even remotely in prospect. Zara and I laughed about it, eventually, and I told her it probably wouldn't be long before they started guessing that she was pregnant.

Over time, I learned to resign myself to the attentions of the photographers, sometimes even to marvel at their perseverence and ingenuity. Random pictures of us together were always being taken and some of them actually came out well. Much of the time, inevitably, they caught us off guard and, on such occasions, read something into an expression that simply wasn't meant. Zara knows you cannot beat them, or drive them off the scent, so there is no point in getting upset, but it is not something you could ever come to enjoy.

The worst episode we endured in our time together was the Sunday newspaper story alleging we'd had a violent row on a night out in Oxford. A group of us had gone out, the previous Saturday evening, and because we were likely to have a few drinks, we paid someone to drive us there and back. We knew the bloke quite well, as he used to drive Warren Marston to the races when he lost his licence for a speeding offence, but if I say that none of us has seen or heard of him since that night, you can guess the rest. He had gone to the newspaper and offered them a dodgy story. I've no idea how much money they paid him but I am quite sure it was a lot more than he would have got for driving jockeys around for the next year. I still struggle to come to terms with the idea of anyone, let alone a trusted acquaintance, picking up grubby money for a spot of elaborate fabrication. In fact the whole concept of newspapers splashing out money on such people, and such unsubstantiated tales, horrifies me. Subsequently, I heard about others in our circle who have been approached and offered money to 'tell tales' about Zara and me. There were many such offers made after our split but, to my knowledge, all were refused. Someone will take the money every week, however, and, on this occasion, we were the casualties. Zara and I could barely believe it when the paper's story was pointed out to us a week later, and we could also barely recognise ourselves within the article. It was not nice to read, for any of us. Suffice it to say that what actually happened that night is between the group of us who were there but it bore little resemblance to what was printed, as might be indicated by the fact that we all remained close friends, bar the driver who sold his soul.

In the days following that story, we were hounded as never before. On the Sunday, when it first appeared, we went for a roast lunch at The Plough, where the matter was a subject of amused debate. When we came out, photographers were all over the road outside. They parked outside the house later, which really agitated me, and there were journalists with them pressing us for a comment whenever either one of us appeared. It seemed a pathetic charade, really, a comment on the tittle-tattle society these papers breed. A day or two later, I had to laugh at the ingenuity of one of the photographers, though. Things had quietened down, the pack had moved on to hound some other target and this chap had turned up outside the house by himself. To avoid looking obvious, he drove a few yards past, then lifted the bonnet and pretended to be tinkering with the engine. The cameras on the back seat were a bit of a giveaway, though.

Thankfully, life was not always like that. We really did not feel we were in a goldfish bowl all the time, largely because of the area in which we chose to live and the things we chose to do. We were not out on the town every night - neither of us has the energy, let alone the inclination, left for that - and, when we did go out to eat, it was either with friends or in one of the pubs where we were known. Pubs were fine, anonymous boltholes, I found, and I felt no restrictions on where we should be seen together in that sense. Our circle of friends was large, not only from the racing community but from Zara's own sporting activities in hockey and eventing.

She plays hockey for Cheltenham and I went to watch once, but it seems a lethal game to me and I can't think why girls play it. They do seem to know how to enjoy themselves afterwards, though. The eventing has become a far more serious part of Zara's life now and I encouraged her to take as much responsibility for the horses as she can, because that way it becomes so much more fulfiling. While we were together, she kept her three horses five minutes' drive from home, at the livery yard run by the ex-jockey Chris Maude and his wife, Dolly. It kept Zara extremely busy - she was up to feed them at 6.30am and, whatever else she did with them during the day she would be back there in mid evening to put their rugs on for the night. She is a very good rider and won a prestigious event at Bramham, in Yorkshire, last summer, so hopefully she will continue climbing the ladder in the years to come. I did go to watch her whenever I could but I wish I had had the time to be more supportive. Despite the equine comparisons, our two sports are very different and I found I wandered around at an event with barely anyone knowing who I was. The time on my hands while waiting for Zara to ride, though, was seldom good for my diet, as I ended up stuffing myself from the fast-food stalls.

Zara is determinedly independent and down to earth, which is part of what drew me to her in the first place. She is happy to work as hard as anyone else and she wants to lead a normal life, though inevitably has to put up with a lot of scrutiny. I spent plenty of time with her mother and really enjoyed talking to her. Just listening to her travel experiences, and her knowledgeable views on any subject you care to mention, puts my own world - which I had imagined to be quite rounded - into perspective. She, too, rode to a high standard, of course, and I've no doubt she is a great help to Zara on that front. The fact is that both of them wish to lead normal lives and it is not wholly possible. If you become a top sportsman, or an actor or pop star, the celebrity syndrome comes to meet you. Royals are born into it. Zara's granny just happens to be the Queen but that doesn't make her any different from the rest of us.

One of the best things she has done, at least from my viewpoint, was to become the figurehead of Cheltenham's 16-24 Club, which encourages young people to come racing. Zara enjoys the atmosphere of racing, though to date she has not been that keen to ride in races, which her mother did. Basically, she likes going as a social outlet and she is a very good face to be promoting the sport to a younger generation than it has traditionally attracted. At the

Cheltenham Festival last season there were a lot more pictures of her in the papers than of me - and I found no cause for complaint in that.

Life, for both of us, was so busy that there was never any danger of us being under each other's feet at home. Probably, the opposite was true and we certainly spent more time apart than many living-in couples. Apart from her eventing horses, Zara has qualified as a human masseur and has recently been doing a horse massage course. With my schedule taking me out of the house early and often not returning me until late, there were days when we scarcely saw each other at all.

After we split, there were stories in the papers that I had upset Zara by being late to her 21st birthday party at Windsor Castle. Yes, I was late but only because I had been doing my job, trying to ride winners at an evening race meeting. I like to think Zara understood that. I am at a stage in life when my career comes before everything else - if that sounds selfish, then I am guilty as charged - but being a jockey is not something you can do without total commitment.

Zara saw me in some bad times, as well as some very good ones, and she was supportive throughout. We did not part after a blazing row - indeed, we remain good friends and I hope that will long be the case. We did not part because of any other person. We decided to part - and it was a mutual decision - because we both still have a lot of living to do. Disregard the royal factor that seems to entrance so many and it should be easy enough to understand that simple explanation.

19.

Mixed emotions
The story of the 2001-2 season

How do you assess a season in which so much went wrong, yet so much unarguably went right? Was I to feel pleased or disappointed, relief or frustration? The answer, I think, is a little of everything. There was a sense, for me, of being on a constant rollercoaster through the winter of 2001-2. Stop it at different stages and I would have been feeling either very high or extremely low. Certainly, it was the most eventful season of my career and I should be satisfied to have finished it with 132 winners, including two at the Cheltenham Festival. How much better it could have been, though, if What's Up Boys had clung on to the Grand National victory that looked to be his, and if Ilico, more than five months earlier, had not fallen - fatally for him and damagingly for me - at Exeter. Yet that is the precarious nature of this sport, the thing that gives it such endless fascination. Horse have to jump safely and gallop extreme distances. Jockeys have to be both tough and fortunate. This was a season that tested out my resilience, physically and mentally.

At the start of the season, I would have included Ilico and What's Up Boys, both trained by Philip Hobbs, in any shortlist of those I was especially looking forward to riding. I ended up regarding them with unimagined emotions. Ilico was gone, a tragic and wasted figure in my season, while What's Up Boys had introduced me belatedly to the true magic of Aintree, the sense of feeling you have won the world's most famous race, and then having it snatched away. Some rollercoaster. Some season.

Such drama seemed a distant prospect when the season began, as is now customary, with the long but spasmodic summer jumping campaign. I know a lot of people in racing did not approve when National Hunt became a 12-month exercise and I can understand the objections, especially by stable staff for whom there was now no obvious time for a holiday. The old, two-month break in June and July did ensure that everybody, jockeys included, took a proper break and came back refreshed in August. With that said, I have no personal complaints about summer racing - on the contrary, I positively relish it, especially now that the meetings have become far more competitive than was once the case. For the first couple of years, summer jumping was of a pretty ropey standard but it has made rapid advances and there are now far fewer easy races to farm. The reason is obvious - plenty of those trainers who did not want it to happen are now having some runners through the summer, while others keep a team specifically for this period, almost as a separate entity in the yard.

I personally feel the summer season does not really start until July. In May, and even June, horses that have been in training through the winter will still be around. It's not like the old days, when a horse was chucked in a field as soon as the season ended. Nowadays, there are plenty of useful horses kept back until May 1, to preserve their novice status, then sent out to try and win a couple of races before being turned out for their summer break. Philip Hobbs is very adept at this. He often buys horses off the flat at the

November sales, possibly giving them a run or two and then, providing they have not won, allowing them a midwinter break before getting them back up again to run through May and June. As he is one of my main providers of rides, along with Henry Daly, Alan King and Richard Phillips, this is a productive system for me.

Spectrometer was a good example of this method. In the summer of 2001, he won three hurdle races on fast ground and was among the horses that contributed most to the fastest start I have made to a season. Mentally, as well as materially, summer jumping has been a help to me. It is a horrible feeling when the winner count winds back to nought at the end of a season and I just can't wait to get off the mark again. May has become a particularly busy month now and although the rides get a little thinner on the ground as the summer proceeds, the extremely valuable races put on by Market Rasen and Uttoxeter help to maintain the level of interest. It is quite something for middle-rank jumps courses to be putting on races worth £50,000 and £60,000 in June and July but the crowds they attract, and the commercial backing, is evidence that the enterprise is being rewarded.

With the volume of racing as it is, and the level of support I have behind me, I feel I can start a season now with 200 winners as a realistic target. Had I stayed fit last season, I would have been disappointed not to do it. Winning the title is never going to be easily attainable so long as McCoy and Pipe remain a team but, as summer became autumn in 2001, I did not see why A.P. should ever be more than 30 winners ahead of me. Kept within those bounds, an injury or a couple of suspensions can then open up all kinds of possibilities. In mid-October, I was actually fewer than 20 adrift, no mean feat considering the ammunition Mr Pipe always reserves for summer, and I recall a sense of excitement, thinking ahead to a winter that promised to be as busy for me as it would be for Tony. Well, that was the theory, anyway.

I was on 81 winners as I drove to Exeter on October 23. A favourite track and a good book of rides, with at least three decent chances, meant that the journey passed in a pleasant blur of anticipation. Ilico was to be my first ride of the day and he was something to savour. He had been bought in France to join the Hobbs yard, so came with plenty of jumping experience, and he was a very good novice hurdler the previous season - Adrian Maguire had actually ridden him to win a decent race at Aintree in which I had opted to partner his stablemate Reiziger. Ilico was a big horse, a ready-made chasing type, and he had done everything asked of him on the schooling grounds. This was to be his debut over fences and, while it was not an uncompetitive race, he was a worthy favourite.

Ilico jumped the first three as I hoped he would, safely and unspectacularly. You do not want a novice to jump extravagantly and there was no sign of it, but neither was there a semblance of a mistake. I was tracking Jim Culloty on one of Henrietta Knight's, knowing it would have been well schooled, and I was content with the way the race was panning out. The fourth was the first ditch and we were literally a couple of strides from it when Jim's horse veered across in front of mine, temporarily blinding him. Not only was Ilico's eye taken off the fence but his mind, as well. It was like a blindfold person running into a stone wall and the result was the same. I knew I was going to fall and, in such circumstances, the split-second left to you is spent offering up a silent prayer for a soft landing.

It didn't happen. Although the ground was on the easy side, cushioning my fall, the horse came down on top of me before rolling back to his feet and galloping off. That was the last I saw of him and, as he had sprung up looking in better health than me, I had no cause to suspect the worst. I did not discover until the following day that he was dead. Apparently, he had galloped about 200 yards from the scene of the fall before collapsing with a brain haemorrhage. It shocked and upset me when I heard this news but, for my own sake, I was mightily relieved he had not suffered the haemorrhage as he came down on top of me. If that had happened, I might not now be happily embarked on another new season.

I have a ritual after a fall. I twitch my arms and legs to re-establish movement and identify what might be sore. There was no blinding flash of pain but I had a sensation that something was very wrong. I tend to go as white as a sheet at the sight of blood and, although there was none evident now, the same feeling overcame me as I realised what I had done. My foot was at an angle and I knew instinctively that a bone in the lower leg had been broken. The single blessing was that Ilico had not mangled it completely as he hit me.

The ambulance staff were quickly clustering round me and one well-meaning man, evidently concerned to discover if I had any head injuries, lent on my leg as he bent to attend to me. I kept saying: "Get off my leg, get off my leg," but it seemed not to register. Eventually, I screamed at him, probably sounding very rude but feeling, by then, panicky that he would make a bad situation even worse. I am never at my best when surrounded in this way after a fall. I feel claustrophobic, anxious for my own air and space. Probably, down the years, quite a few apologies are in order, because these people are only trying to do their best for us. This, though, was the worst injury I've suffered and, in those long minutes lying in the Devon mud, the full impact of it began to sweep over me. Given the circumstances, I hope I can be forgiven if I was impolite.

A jockey has a sixth sense about injuries and I was 90 per cent certain the leg was broken. I know the signs of fractures now. Collar-bones, in particular, grate slightly as you try to move and there was something unpleasantly similar about what I was experiencing now. They lifted me onto a back board, just in case there was any spinal damage, then loaded me into the ambulance which, unfortunately, had to complete almost a full circuit of the racecourse. The track for emergency vehicles was rough and I was bounced up and down, the discomfort levels rising with every pothole. They gave me an injection for the pain but it seemed to make little difference.

One stroke of luck was that 'Rabbit' Slattery was on duty at Exeter. She is the main jockeys' physiotherapist in the south and most of us would trust her implicitly. I retained the presence of mind to ask the doctor if I could see her before the examination proceeded, just for my own reassurance. The next thing I did was ask for a phone so that I could phone Mum. I could picture the scene back at the farm in Herefordshire - Mum is always too nervous to watch a race I am riding in but I was pretty sure Dad would have been looking in, especially as he was well aware of my optimism about Ilico. I knew that if he had seen the fall, she would be fretting, so I wanted to put her mind at rest that I was still alive and kicking. Once she heard my voice, I knew she would be okay, despite the prognosis. Bones mend. Worse things can happen when you come off a horse.

For me, the grimmest hours were still to come. As I was restored to the ambulance for the short journey to hospital in Exeter, the 'why me?' mentality began to kick in. I felt desolate, knowing that

I faced a lengthy spell of inaction and fearing, however irrationally, that the news could be even worse. Briefly, I worried if I would ever be able to ride again.

They treated me very well during my three days and nights in the Royal Devon & Exeter Hospital and I am grateful. However, certain moments will living with me for a long while. The first was in the x-ray room, where I was left for a short while awaiting a doctor. I lay on the bed in the cubicle feeling utterly alone and useless. There was a sense of desolation at that point and I could easily have cried. To cheer me up a shade, three of the lads - 'Choc' Thornton, Ben Hitchcott and Vince Slattery - dropped in to see me after racing and they were with me when the x-ray results confirmed the break. The doctor said he would not be operating on it until the following morning and I was happy with that. I'd had enough for one day. I had not reckoned with what was still to come.

A female nurse told me I needed a light plaster on the leg to keep it straight overnight. She set about this job by picking up my leg, just below the knee, almost as if she had forgotten where the bone was broken. Whether or not it was my fevered imagination, I swear I saw the bone bulge through the skin and I literally screamed out with pain. It was a scream all of Devon might have heard, because it was a pain the like of which I had never known. The nurse carried on, no doubt used to such reactions, and I tried to tell myself that she had to do her job and I simply had to tolerate it. But I couldn't. After a few, very long seconds of agony I had to ask her to stop, whereupon she summoned a male colleague, basically to hold me down. When she started fitting the plaster again, I had hold of this fellow's arm so tight I saw the veins pop up in it. They tried to give me gas and I was taking great, desperate gulps of it, but it made no difference. I'm not sure how I got through those few minutes and I don't think the memory of it will easily go. Like any other jockey, I've learned to live with the certainty that there will be falls and injuries and occasional pain, but I never wish to experience anything like that again. Frankly, I was frightened by the intensity of it. Until it was over, and I could draw breath and start behaving normally again, I had almost forgotten that the lads from the weighing-room were still there, and had witnessed this little scene. Vince has broken his leg, too, and said he knew what I was going through but I think 'Choc' and Ben hardly knew where to look.

Once the treatment stopped, the pain vanished as if by magic. I slept fine, with virtually no discomfort, and soon after waking I was being wheeled down to the operating theatre, consoling myself that nothing could be as bad as what I'd already gone through. And, of course, it wasn't. I didn't even have time to worry about it. I had only once had surgery before and I recalled that when they injected me with the anaesthetic they told me to start counting to ten, warning that I would probably only get halfway. I think I managed 'one, two' before oblivion took over and the same thing happened now. When I came round, Mum, Dad and Zara were at my bedside and I felt extremely lightheaded and incongruously content. "Whatever it is they have given me, I'll have some more," I said dozily.

Initially, I had been put in a large ward that seemed to be inhabited by the very old and extremely ill. It was a sad and depressing place and, thankfully, I was quickly moved to a room of my own. Its amenities included a television but not a telephone - well, not officially, anyway. During that first day, so many friends from the racing fraternity phoned to speak to me that the nurses tired of bringing in the handset from the outside ward and left it with me, telling me to answer any more calls because they were bound to be for me. I had plenty of visitors, too. Philip Hobbs and his wife, Sarah, were among the first and so, touchingly, was Martin Pipe. Considering how little I ride for him, this was quite a gesture but it didn't really surprise me. I have a lot of time for Mr Pipe, both as a fantastic trainer and a very nice person. His son, David, came in separately, as did Jimmy Frost, who has recently started training down in the West Country.

Everyone was being very kind and the hospital staff could not have been nicer, but I still longed to be out of the place. The doctor told me I should be able to go home on the Friday and I meant to make certain they stuck by that. I persuaded one of the nurses to let me up for a shower, not being too keen on the bed bath routine, and the simple process of getting clean under a jet of water has never felt so good. It was a touch of freedom, quite apart from making me feel a little more human.

It was great to get home but boredom kicked in after precisely one day. For two weeks, I was stir crazy, quite unable to come to terms with the enforced inactivity. I have never found it easy to sit still for long - I'd have been terrible working in an office - and the fact that I could now do nothing else began to drive me mad. The physio had shown me how to get up stairs on my crutches, so at least I wasn't completely helpless, but there was no question of driving a car. And so, each afternoon, I settled down in front of the television to watch wall-to-wall racing, tormenting myself by counting the rides I was missing and winners I had lost, and wondering what the lads were up to in the weighing-room. The worst day came about ten days after the accident. It was a Saturday, a decent card at Chepstow, and I watched with sinking spirits as three nice horses that would normally have been my rides won the first three races.

I think that day changed me. The feeling it left me with was so utterly empty that I unconsciously gave up the daily masochism. Gradually, I stopped watching so much racing and stopped fretting over what I was missing. I accepted that there was nothing I could do about it and became steadily more philosophical. The following week I went to Cheltenham, driven by Zara, and despite having only a limited range of movement I really enjoyed seeing everybody again. Already, the most striking catharsis of the whole saga, the increasing awareness of my good fortune in lifestyle, was underway.

The stitches came out in two stages. After the first, I was encouraged to start using a local swimming pool and quickly found I could walk with the water up to my chest and a degree of weight on the bad leg. When the final stitches were removed, I was allowed to drive an automatic car and felt an exhilarating sense of restored freedom. Now, I could get up (though no earlier than a leisurely 9am) and actually plan something I could do during the day. It always included swimming and, soon, a daily visit to the gym - and I watched increasingly fewer races on television.

Some days were still very difficult. On Hennessy Gold Cup day at Newbury, I was recruited by BBC television to do some punditry. It is probably not my forte anyway but I found myself getting especially tongue-tied after watching Behrejan lead until a few strides from the line before having the prize snatched from him by What's Up Boys. If fit, I would have been able to choose between these two horses as my ride in the race and I am still not sure now which one I would have picked. Perhaps injury saved me from the frustration of getting it wrong, as I always believed What's Up Boys was a better horse in the second half of a season.

A week later at Sandown, there was no doubt that I would have been on the winner of the Tingle Creek Chase, yet as Flagship Uberalles romped home I was at least pleased for Robert Widger, who rode him in my place. Robert is a lovely lad who has worked at Minehead for Philip Hobbs for five years or so. He is a good schooling jockey and a very competent race rider, as he showed that day, but his name has never become fashionable, the chances have not come his way and, gradually, disillusionment has set in. Even that big winner was not enough to reverse the trend and, when the season ended, Robert began talking of retirement. His weight is a big problem and he no longer had the will or incentive to conquer it, so decided to return to his native Ireland, where he would be able to resume riding as an amateur.

So, two valuable winners on successive Saturdays for the Hobbs stable and I had missed them both. My consolation was that Philip had not gone outside the yard for his jockeys (Paul Flynn had partnered What's Up Boys, as he did when he won at the Cheltenham Festival in 2000), so there should be little opposition to my getting back on them. The frustration was gnawing at me, nonetheless, so when Zara came up with the idea that we should go to Australia for a holiday, it did not take long to see the benefits. I had never been before and, injury apart, there seemed no prospect of having the time to undertake such a trip until I stop riding. It was too good an opportunity to miss and it did me good in a sense.

We left on Boxing Day (ironically, after seeing another big winner slip by when Adrian Maguire replaced me on Florida Pearl in the King George) and we were there a little over a fortnight. It was now more than two months since the leg was broken and I was getting close to fitness. I took one crutch with me but discarded it almost as soon as I got there. We did plenty of cycling and swimming and, during the second week, I spent a lot of time in the gym. The hot weather, I found, was good for the leg, though I had not been so sure after the first couple of days. The area around the wound was getting unnaturally warm, the remaining callouses seemed to be swelling and I got worried about the possibility of an infection. Fortunately, we were staying with James Erskine, whose company Zara had worked for on a previous visit to Sydney. James had been to medical school, and failed, but a doctor friend was also staying in the house and, having taken a look at the leg, he reassured me that this was simply a sign of the body working overtime in my interests, the mending process being accelerated by the sun.

We arrived home on January 13 and I would love to have been back in action at the end of that week, as Looks Like Trouble was making what turned out to be a successful comeback at Wincanton. The combination of two crocks returning together seemed a romantic yarn but it would not have been fair to anyone concerned to rush back after investing so much time and effort in getting fit. I stifled my impatience, watched the Wincanton race on TV, and the following Tuesday kept an appointment with my specialist, who agreed (having spoken on the phone to the Jockey Club doctor, Michael Turner) that I could start riding immediately. I came out of that room feeling mightily relieved and got straight on to Dave Roberts to find me a horse.

Dave, characteristically, kept my feet on the ground. He pointed out that the major mid-season races were past, the jockeys' title race had long since been decided and that my priority should be to peak for Cheltenham without any further setbacks. He suggested that we did not look to ride anything and everything but concentrate on my regular stables, taking only those spares that had an obvious chance of winning. At times like this, Dave is more manager than agent.

Considering he takes a slice of every riding fee I earn, he was advising me against his own short-term interests, but both of us knew that it made sense within the bigger picture.

Thursday January 24, three months and a day after Ilico's fall, was to be the big day and the choice of meetings was Warwick and Plumpton. Slightly to my surprise - Warwick being both more local to me and a track that my usual trainers customarily target - Dave rang on the Wednesday morning to say he had found the ideal ride for me, in the selling hurdle at Plumpton. Comebacks do not come much lower-key than that. He was right, though, it was an ideal ride. At the age of ten, Balanak had been around for so long he knew a good deal more about the game than most of the people riding him and the one thing I knew for certain was that he would provide an immediate test of my strength and persuasion.

Dave had phoned Balanak's trainer, David Gandolfo, to ask for the ride and, despite having made a provisional arrangement elsewhere, he was good enough to oblige. I drove down to East Sussex that morning feeling unusually nervous. Three months is a long absence, for any jockey, and I was nagged by irrational self-doubt. Would I be able to get back quickly to where I was before? Would the same people still give me rides? Will the leg stand the strain? And so on. With so much apprehension, it seemed a long journey, though I was at Plumpton almost before the course officials, such was my eagerness to get started. I did a few press interviews, then settled slowly back into an enjoyment of the weighing-room atmosphere, even if much of the banter and wisecracking was mischievously directed my way. On the way out, a few cameras were fired in my face and a lot of spectators wished me luck, all of which helped to reassure me that I had not been forgotten while I was away.

The ride was everything Dave had predicted it would be, a thorough work-out which gave me a decent gauge on how far I had come, and still had to travel. On soft ground, Balanak was always going to be hard work and I had to push him most of the way round this undulating track. Halfway round the final bend, I felt my chest burning, a sure sign that I was short of work. The trainer was happy enough, though, and the racecourse presented me with a bottle of champagne - the only one I ever expect to get after finishing fifth in a seller.

The relief at having taken this first step back to normality was immense, but now I had to begin the serious business of riding winners again, and that took a while to kick-start. I drew a blank at Doncaster the following day, then had several good chances at the big Saturday meeting at Cheltenham. None of them won, though I rode two seconds which reintroduced me to the fickle world of gullible punters. After Legal Right was runner-up in the Pillar Chase, a man ran down to the horsewalk and shouted some congratulations at me. Perhaps he had backed it each-way. Later, when I had finished second again on Rooster Booster in the handicap hurdle, the same bloke appeared in the same spot, this time hurling abuse at me and shouting that I was crooked. It made me laugh, even if the feeling was hollow. Did he really think that any sane jockey would stop a horse when he had not ridden a winner for more than three months?

I got back on the scoreboard on the Monday after my return, riding a double at Kempton, and felt hugely the better for it. My first target was to complete 100 winners for the season, a significant milestone for any jockey, and in the course of the next few weeks I chipped away at that aim while steadily getting back to full fitness and sharpness in the saddle. Cheltenham, the primary focus of the season for everyone involved in jump racing, increasingly dominated my thoughts and, as the days ticked away, I kept a mental tally of the rides I had secured and the races in which I was still available - it was still Dave's job, of course, but for that one week of the year every jockey is keenly aware of each and every opportunity for glory.

On the Saturday before Cheltenham I had the kind of day that examines the mental stability of a jockey. I went to Chepstow with a book of rides that anyone would envy - seven in all, and I was quietly confident that the first three should win. Somehow, all three got beaten and after the third setback, walking back up the long flight of steps from paddock to weighing-room, I felt like giving up for the day and going home. Fortunes have a strange habit of levelling out, though, and I was pretty quickly feeling ashamed of such silent defeatism as two winners were added to my score by the end of a day on which Adrian Maguire was ruled out of Cheltenham (and way beyond) for the umpteenth time. I went home counting my blessings, knowing I had only one more raceday to survive before presenting myself for duty at the National Hunt Olympics.

The fates did not spare me completely. I was sound of body through the week but my health was deteriorating as a heavy cold took root. Being short of breath and energy is not ideal at the Festival and I coughed my way through the final day feeling sufficiently tired and rough to have taken a day off if I had been in another place, or maybe in another job.

Cheltenham went well for me, though. I can always pick holes, identify areas of disappointment, but any jockey must be satisfied to come away with two winners from the meeting, one in a feature race and the other, on the previously luckless Rooster Booster, in the final heat of the meeting - the perfect way to end. Flagship

Uberalles was always my likeliest winner of the week and there is relief, as well as elation, when the bankers come in. Though the rest of my rides that day ran below par, it hardly mattered. Even a whip ban for excessive use on Flagship, which many observers deemed harsh, did not spoil my sunny outlook on life. In the strictest analysis, I had broken the rules, so there could be no logical argument.

The suspension, allied to a few days with no jump racing scheduled, opened a window for another mini-holiday and, at the promptings of Zara, we went skiing. To say we did this together is perhaps an exaggeration. Zara has been skiing all her life and is very proficient, leaving me behind. I've only been a few times and it took me a while get back into the rhythm of it. Even when I did, I would have won few points for style.

After Cheltenham, of course, the next big thing in the jumping season is Aintree, yet this has never been a favourite course for me and the National had never been a favourite race. In fact, as I had never managed to complete one, I regarded the whole thing with a healthy contempt that could only be altered by the kind of experience I was about to have.

I had reached a stage of frustration with the National where I just wanted to get it over with each year. I always seemed to fall early on and I now expected nothing else. Perhaps that helped me on this occasion, because instead of trying to worry my way through all the potential pitfalls I just went out to enjoy myself. Carl Llewellyn says he approaches it that way and he has won it twice, so he must be doing something right. The key, though, is that you need a horse that enjoys the peculiar demands of Aintree and actually wants to jump those fences. Leading up to the race, I was not at all sure that What's Up Boys fitted that description.

What Aintree has done very successfully is enhance the quality of the rest of its three-day meeting. In years gone by, most of the support cards were dross and window-dressing; the National was all that mattered. Now, there is serious prize money and highly competitive fields, and while I still have severe misgivings about the Mildmay course, in particular, I have nothing but praise for the environment of the meeting and the atmosphere generated in the course.

For we southern jockeys, it is one of the few meetings each year when we stay away. It makes no sense to do a five-hour round trip each day and there is also a lively Liverpool social scene to enjoy in the evenings. With no requirement to get up early and ride out, it is possible to have an evening out without compromising work, and I found myself riding at a leisurely hour on Friday and Saturday mornings before meeting up with a number of jockeys who did not look to be feeling quite as well as me.

Friday is the day when the city descends on the racecourse and it becomes a massive works outing. The weather was unseasonally warm, which meant that the girls were wearing very little and that even more booze than usual was drunk. By the time racing had finished, there were some memorable sights among the reluctantly home-going spectators, yet despite the state many of them were in I noticed no sign of anything bar good-natured exuberance. Long may it stay that way.

There was a fair bit of exuberance among the jockeys that night, too, much of it the result of pre-National nerves. Friday had brought me a varied return, with In Contrast winning the big novice hurdle and Gower-Slave falling in the Topham Trophy over the National fences. In Contrast has huge ability but hangs badly, so when the chance presented itself to get past the leader on the rail on the turn into the straight, I had to take it. That leader was Westender, ridden by one A.P.McCoy, and it would be fair to say that the jockey was not very happy at my manoeuvring up his inner, and let me know his feelings on the matter. I'm sure it won't worry either of us for long. Gower-Slave had won the Topham the previous year but on much softer ground. With the course drying so fast this year, the pace was hectic and he had a typical Aintree fall, overjumping at Bechers Brook and pitching forward as he landed. I bruised my back painfully enough to give up my final ride as a precaution but my main concern as I left the course was to something similar happening the next day. I wasn't convinced that What's Up Boys would take to those fences. He is a small horse, had a lot of weight to carry and, surrounding myself with a protective pessimism, I considered it would be a minor miracle if we got round safely. It just shows how wrong you can be.

Jockeys are often going on about the deprivations they face in order to keep their diet in check. Friday night in Liverpool found me bucking the trend. Having had a drink or two with some owners, and then found the evening more advanced than I expected, I opted for a healthy burger in MacDonalds at 10.30pm. Back at the hotel, where many jockeys were staying, the bar was lively long into the night but I was up in good time on Saturday and, against my usual instincts, edgily looking forward to the big race.

Even if you have steeled yourself to be neutral about the National, it takes you over long before the tapes rise. The buzz in the weighing-room is of a higher intensity than on any other day, jockeys are wishing each other luck and plainly meaning it, and then, when you step out into the crowd, the walk to the paddock is halted every few yards by people asking for souvenir autographs. It has always bewildered me that anyone should want mine, not least because it is indecipherable, but I gladly scrawled it out a dozen or so times before joining the Hobbses and their owners in the parade ring. Frankly, I was petrified. I do not get this nervous before any other race but, no matter my ambivalence about the National, it churns a jockey's emotions year after year.

At the start, I found myself lining up next to Warren. Instead of wishing him luck, I just shouted that I hoped he stayed in one piece. Then we were off, charging down the long run to the first as happens every year. My horse jumped it well, and prominently enough for me to be unaware of the carnage behind me, in which almost a quarter of the field came down. Not that this would have worried What's Up Boys. Mocking all my pre-race fears, he seemed to love the challenge of the course and whenever another horse fell, he would be nimble and quick-witted enough to avoid it without losing momentum. He seemed to be finding it fun and, against all my instincts, I even began to enjoy it myself.

The National is not won on the first circuit, though it can easily be lost, so I was content to fiddle away in midfield, just letting the horse do his own, increasingly confident, thing. Once we had negotiated The Chair, in front of the heaving stands, then the water-jump, I began to pay more attention to position. At the fence formerly known as Foinavon, a grey horse of Sir Stan Clarke's, Gun'n'Roses, ploughed through the obstacle and hit the deck right in front of us, but my horse took two neat side-steps and galloped on without pause or panic. This was a seriously rare attitude and I began to realise at that point that he had a chance.

We were still ten lengths off the lead but the rest of the race then took shape as if in a dream sequence. I'm sure we did not quicken our pace but other runners kept dropping back past us, fatigue getting the better of them. We jumped Canal Turn well and I decided to stay in the middle of the track, keeping away from potential trouble as much as possible. We were up with the leaders now and experience had taken me over, so that I had forgotten what race it was and found I could concentrate without pressure. What's Up Boys came off the bridle after the third last and, across the Melling Road, I thought we were beaten. The sight of the straight, and the crowds massed ahead of him, seemed to give him a second wind, though, and when he flew the second-last it dawned on me that the Grand National, one of sport's most celebrated prizes, was suddenly there to be won.

I surprised myself by letting him go long again at the last but he jumped it boldly. Bindaree, having led us into the straight, made a mistake and I got a length or two up. At the elbow, I thought I'd won and every available emotion began seeping into my head. Then, just as suddenly, I felt my horse droop beneath me, as if his entire body was shutting down and there was nothing more he could give. I tried to get him closer to the far rail, to help him concentrate, but he was rolling right-handed, drunk with the effort, and the last thing I wanted to do was yank his head around at this stage. Out of the corner of my left eye, I saw Jim Culloty and Bindaree rallying, with the rail to run against. One last effort, one final try to lift my horse over the line, but it was still too far away. After four-and-a-half miles, the race was 50 yards too long.

Previous years had been easy, compared to this. At least when you fall before the race is half done, you have no chance to dream. I think I knew what it was like to win the National, yet now I had to accept that it had passed me by. My first feeling was disbelief, then anguish as I told myself I would never have a better chance. Nobody wants to know the runner-up, in the National or any other race, and I wandered back into the weighing-room in a state of shock.

Usually, the best bit of the National is the gathering of jockeys afterwards, swapping stories as they watch the re-run of the race on the weighing-room television. Now, as I gazed at the screen, seeing my horse clear on the run-in, I fleetingly thought there had been some mistake and that I would see now that I had won, after all.

Later, with no sense of hurry to leave the scene, I went for a drink with 'Choc' Thornton, then slowly headed back to the car park. The first people I saw were Nigel Twiston-Davies and Raymond Mould, the winning trainer and owner. Nigel had stunned the press conference afterwards by saying that he planned to retire from training but this result had changed everything. He is not very adept at dealing with public scrutiny but I have always found Nigel a nice, misunderstood man. That evening, he looked as confused as I felt. Raymond offered me a drink, which I declined, and then asked if I had room in my car to take a package back home, as his vehicle was full. He gave me a box and I asked what was in it. 'The trophy', he said. So there I was, the first Grand National runner-up in history to be driving off with the winner's trophy.

I even attended the Bindaree party, helping to drink away some of Nigel's profits at the Hollow Bottom pub in Naunton village, and by Sunday I was suffering with a double hangover - one from too much drink, the other from the seeping frustration of the experience. I had left my car at the pub and when I popped back there at lunchtime, the horse's homecoming was in full swing. After half-an-hour in which everyone I met wanted to say 'bad luck', I had to get away. It was a strange, mixed-up weekend, but I am quite certain I will look forward to the National more ardently next year.

On the Monday, I drove to Kelso for one ride. A ten-hour round trip and the horse was beaten. It sounds insane and, when it brings no reward, you obviously question the point of it. But I have always been prepared to travel anywhere for the chance of a winner and it is a matter of pride and professionalism to go on doing so. I know that more clearly than ever from something that happened a few weeks later.

The 2001-2 season had ended at Sandown, with the Attheraces meeting. Though I had no winners there, I finished with a score that satisfied me. I had set myself a target of 50 winners after my comeback and I rode 51. It was a relief to feel I was back at the level I had fought to attain, because time moves on and it is so easy to be forgotten. People talk about who rode the winners today, not yesterday or the day before and certainly not three months ago. I was happy with the way I had come back from the most serious injury of my career but now I had to stay there, to start all over again with the scoreboard reading nought. The first day of the 2002-3 season, two days after Sandown, got me off the mark but the following day I decided against driving to Hexham for a single ride. When it won, I was absolutely mortified. I could not believe I had sacrificed a winner through idleness. I won't make that mistake again.

20.
What next?

Racing has an image problem with much of the general public. There is no point in any of us within the sport denying it. Some outsiders regard racing just as a seedy exercise for addicted punters and many more believe that there is constantly something crooked going on. You hear it said everywhere. If I am in the company of a group of people with no involvement in the sport, it is a safe bet that they will pretty soon ask what I think about John McCririck - they may not know his name but they will know him as the most instantly and widely recognised face of racing - and then they will make some crack about racing being bent.

There is an argument that no-one need worry, for racing has always played the sleaze card to its advantage. Dick Francis has had a considerable influence on this, just as Damon Runyon and his low-life American racing characters did, many years earlier. It is a fact of life that people relish the idea of a little chicanery, often because they feel that if there are insiders 'in the know', then maybe they can join them. It never ceases to astonish me how frequently I get calls on my mobile phone, usually from people I may have met only once or twice, asking me about my rides for the day ahead as if I am sure to be in a position to tell them which will definitely win. My job would be very different, and a whole lot less pressured, if I really knew that. If, in an effort to cut the conversation short, I mention an odds-on shot they seem to go away smugly content, believing they have gained some vast advantage over the poor saps who just sit down, look at the form and conclude that my horse has a better than even chance of winning. The whole thing is beyond me - it is not as if jockeys, as a breed, are any good at tipping.

It is harmless enough for people to delude themselves in this way, of course, but in a sense they are all in thrall to the idea that racing is corrupt. A couple of controversial BBC television programmes last summer, 'Kenyon Confronts' and 'Panorama', did nothing to dispel the notion. In fact, they did quite the opposite, doubtless convincing many more viewers that it is a fundamentally dodgy sport. Well, I am sorry to disappoint all those who may be awaiting scandalous revelations from me, but I think the image of racing is both unfair and inaccurate. Of course, there are characters on the borders of the sport that have dishonest intentions - gambling, I am afraid, attracts them like an irresistible magnet. But, from my admittedly limited experience (and I must pass over the specific case of Brian Wright and his gang without comment, because I know only what I have read about him), the influence they have on events out on the course is generally negligible.

I saw one TV programme that seemed to allege that horses are being 'stopped' in virtually every race that is run. This was news to me, and I think it will have startled most of the jockeys I know, because it simply isn't true. I can only speak for myself in this matter but I have been riding for eight years now and I have never once been asked to 'stop' a horse. Perhaps it's because of my style, and the crooks just think that I ride so vigorously it would be obvious if I wasn't doing my best. Perhaps they know I would be contemptuous, because I live to win races, not to throw them away. I prefer to think, though, that I am in the vast majority on this matter and that the closest most jockeys have come to the seamy side of racing is within the pages of a Francis novel.

I am not blind to what has gone on in the past and what, to some extent, still occurs. It seems clear that there have been jockeys willing to do almost anything for money, which is sad both for them and for the reputation of racing. It is also undoubtedly true that there are horses that are run in races with no intention of trying to win. Occasionally, this may be as part of some elaborate handicap plot of the type highlighted by 'Kenyon Confronts', though I tend to think that the trainers who get involved in attempted coups must learn pretty quickly how seldom they can be successfully executed. Usually, though, the reason is that a horse is either being brought back from injury, tried over a new trip or simply being run as part of the educating process. The Rules of Racing state that every horse must be run on its merits but that does not rule out the many times when a trainer will send a horse racing knowing it cannot win, simply through inexperience. That is a long way from being crooked, though sensationalist reporting may ask the public to believe the worst in everything.

As a jockey, young and raw horses can sometimes put you in a quandary. The first three or four runs of a horse's life will stay with him forever and have a serious influence on his constitution and attitude. If he enjoys them, he is likely to thrive, but if he is put under undue pressure before he is mentally and physically able to respond, it will almost certainly sour him against the game and he will never run to his full potential. Jockeys, as well as trainers, have to weigh up the long term at times. So I never use a stick on a horse running in the flat races we know as 'bumpers' - at least, not unless the horse has already run in several and is now contesting one of the championship 'bumpers' at Cheltenham or Liverpool.

This sensible policy is still fraught with potential hazards. If some punter has backed your 'bumper' ride and you finish second without resorting to the whip, he is going to think you were not trying hard enough. Occasionally, the stewards are going to take a similar view. I never want to be too hard on a young horse, even when he ventures over hurdles, but the stewards have as fine a line to tread as the jockeys. Sometimes, I have been asked why I gave a horse an apparently easy time, when if I had hit it three or four times they would have had me in for use of the stick. It is a very difficult balance for all of us to resolve and it gives endless scope for those who wish to draw the murkiest conclusions.

From my point of view, though, the very thought of setting out to lose a race rather than to win it is a complete anathema. I want to be remembered for my successes in this game and I like to think that if I ever got desperate for money I would get out and do something different rather than try to make a few quid by selling my soul to bent punters. Thankfully, the same attitude applies to all the trainers with whom I have had close working relationships.

This is such a competitive sport for us all, these days. Every jockey wants to be associated with a winning stable, so that his name is in the spotlight and on the shortlist when a good job comes up. Trainers have to meet their targets of winners each year, not just for self-satisfaction but to keep themselves in the shop window for the new owners that will sustain the viability of the yard and its facilities. And owners, too, want success - usually more quickly than it can be obtained. There are those whose only interest seems to be in having a bet but the sensible ones soon realise that if you fiddle round with a racehorse with one big day in mind, it is still more than likely to get beaten when that day arrives - they are not machines and will never win to order. The potential for horses being 'stopped', by one means or another, has also been greatly reduced by the advent of patrol cameras on part of the course, and of dope tests straight after the race.

Having started riding with the cameras already in place, I can only imagine what went on in the past, out of sight from the stands and stewards' box. There are racecourses that are almost designed for such malpractice - Cartmel, where the runners dive into a thickly protected wood before emerging in the home straight, and Warwick, where half a mile of the track is entirely out of sight behind a hill, are obvious examples. Nowadays, though, every move is tracked and filmed - and, for the integrity of the sport, that is exactly how it must be.

The most recent instance of a horse being doped came last spring, and it was trained by Philip Hobbs. Ashgar, by strange coincidence, was 'got at' on the same course - Plumpton - and at the same Easter Bank Holiday meeting as one of the previous, high-profile cases some years earlier (involving a Josh Gifford horse called Lively Knight) that led to a police investigation and the messy, botched arrests of several racing personalities. The Ashgar case seems to have been isolated, however, and it is such a rarity now because it is so easily detected by the testing procedures. Philip was quite upset by the revelation but nobody in their right mind would have thought he was in any way in involved. I know of no-one in racing more competitive than him and he puts so much work into trying to win races, at every grade, that he is not going to stick a needle into one of his horses to make it go slower. Somebody did it, though, which just reinforces the sad certainty that there are some very unscrupulous people on the fringes of the racing industry. No matter what new regulations are introduced, I fear we will never get them all out of the arena. Gambling is just too addictive a draw.

Stories of sleaze and corruption within racing are the lifeblood of the media and the bane of the regulators at Portman Square. To be truthful, they do not greatly bother the jockey fraternity. Unless one of our own is unfairly implicated, there is some salacious pleasure had from debating the latest gossip in the weighing-room because, for almost all of us, such activities simply don't register as being relevant to our lives. It is as if they are happening in a different sport, a different world. They belong to the tabloids while we still only inhabit the *Racing Post*. Of course, it would be irresponsible not to recognise the potential for crime within racing and the dangers it could present, both to individual jockeys and trainers and to the reputation of the sport with the general public. But it is not a daily anxiety to most of us jockeys, because it doesn't come near to touching us.

The fickle behaviour of punters, though - now that does get to us in a big way. We seldom need telling when we are having a bad day, and most of us feel plenty aggravated enough after being beaten on a short-priced favourite, but that does not prevent some of the louder, loutish losers venting their anger and empty pockets on us. In my experience, the genuinely big punters know how to lose with grace - or at least how to smile through clenched teeth - and the worst behaviour usually comes from those who might bet only 10 or 20 on a race and yet, in many cases, cannot afford to lose it. When they do, as will happen more often than not, they flail around for someone other than themselves to blame and the jockey is invariably the most convenient target.

This is another side of gambling that can give racing a bad name and much the worst incident I have seen occurred at Leicester a few years back. Norman Williamson was riding a well-backed horse for Kim Bailey and had the race in the bag after the last flight. Twenty yards from the line, thinking there was no possible danger, he dropped his hands and allowed his horse to coast. You can guess what happened next. Another horse was flying up the run-in and, by the time Norman sensed the danger, it was all too late. He was caught on the line and all hell broke loose among the betting fraternity. To be fair to the aggrieved punters, this was an extreme case and it did look bad. Norman's horse was so decisively the best that anyone who had backed it could have been excused for counting his winnings once he had cleared the last, and for feeling pretty upset at having to rapidly revise the budget. Norman had no excuses. He knew it was a blunder, a rare error of judgement, and he would doubtless have given his riding fee to rewind the tape and ride the horse out to the line. But it was done and there was no taking it back.

Such philosophy did not satisfy those with losing tickets and they gathered like a seething mob as Norman returned, looking suitably shamefaced, to unsaddle in the runners-up spot. The verbal hostility was as bad as I have known in this country but some of the most hostile punters seemed inclined to take it farther and hung around outside the weighing-room looking threatening. Norman wisely escaped out of the back exit and I suspect he was very glad to get in his car and drive away. Yes, he had messed up (and he suffered for it with a fine and a ban) but that is a long way from making him the crook that these punters were painting him. If he had seriously set out to stop that horse from winning, and to deprive them of their betting returns, did they really think he would make such a spectacle of himself by sitting up in the saddle just a few strides from the line?

To a thankfully lesser extent, we all suffer from the frustrations of mug punters and we must all learn to live with it. Gambling owners are another trial. For a young, impressionable jockey, it can be quite an ordeal to stand in the paddock before a race and have your owners tell you that they have had several thousand pounds on the horse and would be pleased if you could do the business for them. There is enough to think about in a race without that kind of pressure. Nowadays, I let it all wash over me. I give no special attention to owners that want to brag about their betting and, while I would far rather not know, I simply don't allow it to affect the way I ride a horse. Down that road, madness lies.

Nerves are another factor for any jockey. We all have them, to a greater or lesser degree, and it may be surprising to some that they get no better with age and experience. Sometimes, in fact, it works the opposite way. The great thing about youth is that you have no fear. When I began race-riding, I surfed along on a tide of enthusiasm and bravado. I didn't really worry about being beaten because I was so seldom expected to win and the cavalier style of my riding probably led to quite a few needless falls. These days, I am not in a muck sweat before any race, with the possible exception of the Grand National, but I have a degree of apprehension before them all, largely because there are now high expectations of me (not least from myself) and I get anxious not to mess things up.

A touch of apprehension before a race is a good thing, in my view. To be too confident and relaxed is to ask for trouble. This is a different matter, though, from the nerves that turn into fear. Jump racing is a dangerous sport, and it did not take a broken leg to impress that upon me. But, while we all have to be aware of the perils and to take as many precautions as are sensible, we cannot let the worst-case scenario rule our thoughts. If we did, we would never get on a horse in the paddock again. It is no different from the world of Formula One, where the driver need nerves of steel to keep going out and duelling at 200mph. If that nerve wavers, and they begin to think more of the risk factor, it is time to get out and do something else. The same applies to those of us who make our living by riding horses over hurdles and fences. We are going to fall regularly, we are going to get injured occasionally, but the physical concerns must never outweigh the desire to go out and ride.

You can see this happening at times, and it is a sad process to observe when the jockey concerned refuses to acknowledge the red-light signals and pack up while the going is good. I am personally of the view that the bravest of horses often lose their bottle quickest. Morcelli, a dazzling grey horse trained in the far north by Howard Johnson, was the most spectacular jumper of fences and seemed to have no fear whatever, yet one day he seemed to decide he just couldn't do it anymore. The problem is that horses cannot tell you this in words. Jockeys can, though, and if ever I recognise the symptoms of failing nerve I hope I admit to it and get out of this addictive but slightly crazy world of ours.

One thing is for sure - I am lucky to be riding in this era, when safety has become such a paramount concern to racecourses and all those who run racing. We have come a very long way in this regard but there is no point in pretending that safety measures will eliminate injuries completely, because it just cannot happen. We are dealing with animals here - big, headstrong and sometimes clumsy animals. There will always be accidents. All we can do is minimise the risk of them becoming serious to man and horse.

Eventing, the other sport that got a constant hearing in my household, has been made safer than ever before, yet a couple of years ago it suffered a bizarre and unrelated sequence of fatal falls.

This had a harrowing effect on everyone involved in eventing and some of them doubtless began to question the whole ethos of the sport. But there was nothing wrong with the obstacles at which these falls occurred and no link was ever discovered. It was bad luck, on a horrific scale, because there is seldom any obvious reason why one person should be seriously injured, or worse, by a fall while another rises unharmed from a very similar tumble.

It is not many years ago that jockeys were going out with flimsy caps and no other protection, to ride on courses where the rails were made of solid metal and the wings of the fences were of jutting timber. It seems remarkable, now, that more jockeys were not maimed in such circumstances. Certainly, I would not fancy going back to those conditions. Helmets have improved significantly even in the time I have been riding, while back protectors are now compulsory for jockeys and made, by two companies, to a standard design. They have done a lot to reduce the risk of spinal damage but, of course, they can never rule it out. In the space of a few weeks, last season, three jockeys quite close to me all suffered serious back injuries. It was said that each of them was lucky not to be left in a wheelchair. Possibly, without the back protectors, that could have been the fate for one or more of them.

It took a surprisingly long time for everyone involved in racing to respond to the risk element and reduce it. Plastic rails, that give and separate in a collision, are a great advance. Doctors are very attentive these days, and anxious that jockeys should not be moved for some while after a heavy fall. Physios are becoming standard on most courses - not before time. Most racecourses are very good on such matters now and the climate of scrutiny is such that they know their standards cannot drop. If they have a fatality on their territory, they have a long time to live with it. Richard Davis died at

Southwell a good few years ago now, but people still remember it. Jockeys naturally discuss safety measures a good deal, comparing the efforts made by different courses. In our line of work, though, it does not do to dwell too long on the potential for injury and most of our daily gripes are reserved for the more functional requirements of our life, such as showers, saunas and sandwiches. A lot of new weighing-rooms have been built in recent years, which is naturally a welcome development, but it is an irritant to us all that some of the courses, given an opportunity to start afresh, have still got it wrong. I don't think we are a particularly demanding breed of people. Our basic desires are to have enough space to change in, more than one properly working shower and a sauna that can accommodate more than two people at a time. Oh yes, and food that pays more attention to the dietary demands of our work than pasties and chips. I don't think that sounds too excessive, yet some courses still find it is beyond them.

A jockey has plenty of time to think about such matters, usually behind the wheel of his car. This is one area of the job that racecourses are powerless to improve and it is commonly accepted as the worst part of our living. I will drive up to 80,000 miles a year and there are days when the process of getting to and from meetings can be completely draining. Often, I will spend six hours or more in the car during a working day and I would hate to know the total hours devoted to driving since I started my career. It is arguably worse for the flat jockeys, during that hectic time of summer when they are trying to do two meetings a day, three or four days a week, but at least they do not have the additional hazards of fog, frost, snow and darkness at both ends of the day. Those who can afford it will often employ a driver - I did so for 18 months and it made such a difference to my quality of life that I am sure I will do so again.

Rushing around can put you in a bad frame of mind for the business of the day. I have only once missed a ride through being late and it was while I was still an amateur - I was heading for Wolverhampton and got stuck in traffic on the M6. That was a good lesson to me and David Nicholson drummed it home, insisting that we should always leave more than enough time to get to the races. Philip Hobbs, who now provides many of my rides, is an example of someone who habitually cuts it as fine as possible, having so much to occupy him at home that he is frequently the last to take the saddle if we have a runner in the first. The trainer, though, does not have to be present - the horse cannot go without a jockey. This is a pressure that can weigh heavy on the cluttered roads of our country and I am often relieved and surprised that there are not more traffic accidents involving jockeys. The only two I have had were in my very early days and came more as a result of being late out of bed and rushing to ride out. I hope they are my last, too.

If these are the ritual moans of our breed, though, they should not camouflage the joys and privileges of the lifestyle. I came to appreciate these so much more during my three months of inactivity last season and I hope it has given me a better perspective on the job. I am one of the lucky ones of jump racing, those who get plenty of rides, ample chances to ride winners. There are probably no more than 15 or 20 us who can make a good living out of the sport and I am lost in admiration for the others, who must really love what they are doing.

Vince Slattery is a great example of a fellow who will go anywhere for just one ride - over jumps or on the flat - and is determined to hang onto his status as a jockey despite the knowledge that he will never break through into the top rank. He is one of the hardest-working jockeys I know and he cannot afford to be choosy about what he rides - I certainly would not want to get on half the horses he does. To augment his earnings, though, Vince is a jack of all trades, who will paint your house, plaster your walls or plumb your toilet in. I was complaining, not long ago, about a loose sink on a wall at my house. Vince piped up that he would come and fix it and, a couple of nights later, he duly appeared on the doorstep. He made a good job of it, too.

If Vince is an extreme example, there are plenty more who simply get by in our game, without ever making or expecting the publicity that has come my way. Some of the best have recently given up, like Gary Lyons, who struggled for years with his weight but had an iron discipline about him, and Robert Bellamy, who lived close to me and was tremendous fun to go racing with. Thankfully, both of them have stayed involved in the sport and we can still enjoy their company.

The camaraderie of the weighing-room is in some ways a cliche but that does not make it any less true. Whatever the success level you are enjoying as a jockey, there is daily contentment in simply being amongst your mates in the very special environment that this sport creates. We celebrate it each year now, at the awards night we call 'The Lesters', a perennial reminder of why we do what we do. This year, they honoured Billy Worthington, a prime example of a nice lad who has worked hard in the game for many years without expecting anything back in the way of perks or privileges. For every one of us who ride 100 winners a season and enjoy the glory of the big days at Cheltenham, there are a score like Billy, enriching the sport with humour and humility long after the good breaks have passed elsewhere.

I have spent a few years now as one of the lucky few, seldom short of rides or winners, but I sincerely hope my career is not yet at its half-way point. I shall not ride into middle-age - I honestly don't think many will in future - but I want to be around for another ten years and I dearly want to evict that McCoy from the champion's throne. To win that title, even once, would be the ultimate fulfilment.